We Knew Mary Baker Eddy

Mary Baker Eddy.

We Knew Mary Baker Eddy

The Christian Science Publishing Society
Boston, Massachusetts, U.S.A.

Steel engraving of Mary Baker Eddy by Jules Maurice Gaspard

Wood engravings by Charles Joslin

Typography and design by Richard Hendel

© *1979 The Christian Science Publishing Society*

Printed in the United States of America

Library of Congress Catalogue Card No. 79-51759

ISBN: 0-87510-115-1

Contents

Foreword   *ix*

A Friendship Through Two Generations   1
by Mary Godfrey Parker

A Worker in the Massachusetts   28
Metaphysical College
by Julia S. Bartlett

The Star in My Crown of Rejoicing—   53
The Class of 1885
by C. Lulu Blackman

Loved Memories of Mary Baker Eddy   63
by Abigail Dyer Thompson

Reminiscences of Mary Baker Eddy   70
by Annie M. Knott

Our Leader as Teacher and Friend   87
by Frank Walter Gale

The Primary Class of 1889 and Other Memories   93
by Emma Easton Newman

The Discoverer and Founder of   102
Christian Science
by Annie Louise Robertson

Contents

The Call to Concord   107
by George Wendell Adams

Recollections of Mary Baker Eddy   111
by John C. Lathrop

The Writings of Mary Baker Eddy   119
by Daisette D. S. McKenzie

An Intimate Picture   127
of Our Leader's Final Class
by Sue Harper Mims

Mrs. Eddy and the Class of 1898   139
by Emma C. Shipman

An Interview with Mary Baker Eddy   146
and Other Memories
by Mary Stewart

Some Precious Memories of Mary Baker Eddy   150
by Calvin C. Hill

Impressions of Our Leader   184
by Bliss Knapp

"With sandals on and staff in hand"   190
by Clara Knox McKee

A Worker in Mrs. Eddy's Chestnut Hill Home   196
by Martha W. Wilcox

Biographical Notes   209

Index   215

Illustrations

Mary Baker Eddy   Frontispiece

                                                              Page

Number 8 Broad Street in Lynn, Massachusetts   3

Mrs. Eddy at State Fair in Concord, New Hampshire   22

The Original Mother Church   49

Chickering Hall in Boston, Massachusetts   64

Birthplace of Mary Baker Eddy in Bow,
New Hampshire   81

Mrs. Eddy's residence at 385 Commonwealth
Avenue, Boston   88

Christian Science Hall in Concord, New Hampshire   100

Pleasant View in Concord, New Hampshire   112

Mrs. Eddy's study in Chestnut Hill   177

Mrs. Eddy's home in Chestnut Hill   198, 199

Foreword

During the latter half of the nineteenth century and the first decade of the twentieth, the figure of Mary Baker Eddy appears on the human scene. Her discovery of the Science that underlay the sacred ministry of the Master, Christ Jesus, and shone through his healing works marks an era of unprecedented change and upheaval in the development of human thought. Mrs. Eddy herself tells us that we find her in her book *Science and Health with Key to the Scriptures* and in her other writings.* These reveal her character and vision and the magnitude of her mission.

There is an inner depth of her nature that is disclosed in a letter to some of her early students: "The spiritual bespeaks our temporal history. Difficulty, abnegation, constant battle against the world, the flesh, and evil, tell my long-kept secret—evidence a heart wholly in protest and unutterable in love.

"The unprecedented progress of Christian Science is proverbial, and we cannot be too grateful nor too humble for this, inasmuch as our daily lives serve to enhance or to stay its glory. To triumph in truth, to keep the faith individually and collectively, conflicting elements must be mastered." **

The reminiscences of some of these early students who were privileged to assist in Mrs. Eddy's home or pioneer in her Church throw a precious light on this inspired Leader. They give us

* See *The First Church of Christ, Scientist, and Miscellany*, p. 120.
** *Ibid.*, pp. 133–134.

glimpses of her colossal strength, her motherliness and tender solicitude; her graciousness, compassion, intuition, wit; her perseverance, adherence to Principle; and, with it all, her untiring love. She looked into realms beyond the temporal and molded her daily life accordingly.

These reminiscences, several of which were originally given as Annual Meeting talks, are taken from the Archives of The Mother Church, The First Church of Christ, Scientist, in Boston, Massachusetts, and were published over a period of years in four small volumes. They have now been arranged chronologically and are presented in this single volume.

L. Ivimy Gwalter

A Friendship Through Two Generations

MARY GODFREY PARKER

When I was about four or five years of age my parents, George Llewellyn and Christiana Godfrey, left their home in Maine to come to Massachusetts where they settled in East Boston. This was around 1873. It was while we lived in East Boston that we became acquainted with Asa Gilbert Eddy.

As I remember, he was an agent for the Singer Sewing Machine Company and went from house to house selling their machines. One day he came to our house and sold a Singer machine to my mother. This was the beginning of his friendship with our family. My mother never disposed of this machine, but because of its associations kept it long after its first usefulness was over.

After that meeting Asa Eddy came regularly to see us. He usually arrived in the late afternoon before I had been sent to bed and always asked for me. Our home was situated so you could see over the hill, and I used to watch patiently at the back windows to catch a glimpse of him so that I could run to the door to meet him. As a child, I did not take to people quickly, but was immediately won to him. Undoubtedly his own fondness for children drew me to him, for he was kind to me and was a jolly playmate in a quiet way, taking me on his knee and entertaining me with all kinds of stories I loved to hear.

I remember so well how he looked, his long black hair, instead of being combed high in a stiff pompadour as shown in his photographs, was brushed back and fell over his left eyebrow in loose curls. There was always a sweet smile on his face and his eyes were so gentle you could not imagine him hurting anything in the world.

All Father's family had been prosperous seamen and respected ship owners in Maine. Father served on his brother's ship before his marriage and traveled far and wide, for a time living in Greenland and Iceland. Father's brothers and cousins were frequent visitors at our home and many were the stirring tales that were told by these sea captains. Our house overflowed with all kinds of relics and mementoes—a regular museum full of interest to anyone.

And so Asa Eddy must have found it, for no one came more frequently or listened more intently than did he when Father and the other men of the family talked over their experiences. Possibly the philosophy of these dauntless seamen appealed to him; for like most New Englanders who sailed the high seas in those days, they were fearless, courageous, honest, God-fearing men, who faced danger in the unshaken confidence that if they did their best and trusted the Lord things would come out all right.

Mother was a very active intelligent woman and came from a long line of eminent Maine people. Many of her family had followed the sea and distinguished themselves. Before her marriage she had taught school and earned a reputation for herself as a woman of culture and ability. It was natural that she should find her friends among those who showed like attributes. It seems to me, therefore, that Asa Eddy must have had an innate refinement and desire for culture and advancement, in order to have made such a strong appeal to her. For though Mother gave much time to charity work among the slums, she was very discriminating and did not admit into her circle of intimate friendship those who were either uncouth or illiterate.

I remember that she used to say that Asa Eddy was such a spiritually-minded man, and as Mother herself was always interested in things of a spiritual nature, this gave them a common meeting ground. Mr. Eddy had great confidence in Mother and used to confide to her many of his hopes and plans. He was not strong,

Number 8 Broad Street, Lynn, Massachusetts

being subject to terrible attacks of illness, which I seem to remember hearing Mother speak of as heart trouble. Because of this
physical disability he was not able to keep at work that confined
him too closely or taxed his strength too much. He wanted to be
healed, but had not been able to find any permanent remedy for
his trouble.

Discouraged because of his poor health, he tried to find some
comfort in religion and investigated the various beliefs current
at that time. Spiritualism was very much before the popular
thought then and both he and Mother looked into it. Though
they used to discuss it a great deal in our home, I know that neither of them ever accepted its doctrines. At that time my family

knew nothing of Mrs. Glover* and her religion, and as far as I know neither did Asa Eddy.

Somewhere around 1875–1876 we moved to Chelsea and Mr. Eddy continued to visit our home there, coming to see us very frequently. It was during our first year there that my mother learned, through her own healing, of the wonderful cures accomplished by Christian Science. She told Mr. Eddy about her experience and urged him to go and see Mrs. Glover.

It came about this way. Mrs. Glover had purchased a house for herself at No. 8 Broad Street, Lynn,** in the spring of 1875 and, needing the extra income, she rented a portion of it. Somehow my mother's favorite nephew, William Nash, who had only been married a year or two and then held an important position in a shoe manufacturing company in Lynn, learned of these rooms and made an arrangement with Mrs. Glover to occupy the second floor, all except the front room which Mrs. Glover reserved for herself.

The Nashes had not been settled very long before Mrs. Nash, who had just had a child, became quite ill and her husband telegraphed my mother to come down. As I was too small to leave alone, Mother had to take me along with her.

At the time Mother was suffering from a badly infected finger, having stuck a needle threaded with green thread deeply into the flesh. She was not one to worry over physical troubles, but when it grew so bad that it became swollen and the doctors said she might lose her arm if she did not have the finger amputated, she grew rather disturbed. She was not willing to submit to such severe measures, however, and tried to stop the putrefaction by applications of tar. This was what she was doing at the time we went to the Nashes.

When we reached the house on Broad Street, we found the Nashes had made arrangements with the owner to serve all her

*Mary Baker Glover Eddy.
**As a result of renumbering, this house is now No. 12 Broad Street.

4

meals. It was at our first meal (supper, as I remember) in their apartment that we met the owner, Mrs. Mary Baker Glover, who came upstairs to the dining room regularly each day to eat with the family. It seems to me, as I look back on it, that my mother may have taken charge of the apartment during Mrs. Nash's illness and looked after the meals at this time. I remember Mother made wonderful pies which Mrs. Glover was particularly fond of. There is a picture in my thought now of Mother working by the sink preparing food of some kind and Mrs. Glover sitting at the table talking to her.

During our first meal together, Mrs. Glover noticed my mother's finger and reached over to touch her hand, asking her what the difficulty was. Mother told her about it and nothing more was said. That night Mother slept through the entire night, the first time in weeks. When she awoke in the morning, the bandage had become unwrapped and fallen off. The finger, which was usually much more swollen in the morning than at any other time during the day, was almost normal.

Mother was frightened and did not know what to make of it. I remember seeing her getting up (we were sharing a room together in the Nashes' apartment) with a little scream and running right out of the room in her nightgown to her nephew and calling out, "Look at my hand." When my cousin William saw it, he said, "Guess Mrs. Glover has been trying her works on it." This did not mean anything to Mother, so he told her what he knew about Mrs. Glover and the sort of healing work she was reputed to do.

That morning at the breakfast table, I think it was, Mrs. Glover again spoke to Mother about her finger, saying, "I will cure it if you will promise not to put anything on it." After what William had told Mother about Mrs. Glover, she realized that possibly here might be a means of help, so she gladly consented and nothing more was said about the finger. Mother discontinued the applications of tar, merely keeping the finger wrapped in a slight bandage, and in eight days' time it was restored to its normal condition, with the exception of some slight malformation of the nail. This persisted until Mother spoke to Mrs. Glover about it a few weeks later; then that, too, was entirely corrected. Of course, Mother was overwhelmed with joy about it and thought Mrs. Glover was the most marvelous woman who ever lived. She was perfectly content just to be with Mrs. Glover and to have opportunity to talk with her.

On this occasion we stayed with the Nashes probably about four to six weeks in the early spring of 1876. (I do not know how long my cousins lived at 8 Broad Street, never having had any record of the dates.) Each day during that time we sat at table with Mrs. Glover. Although the Nashes always had a doctor and a nurse and showed no interest at all in Christian Science, they did respect and admire Mrs. Glover and she felt very friendly toward them and never interfered with them in any way. She was very fond of their little baby girl and named her Flora Glover Nash.

I remember one instance during this visit when Mrs. Glover might have interfered if she had felt inclined. Mother in her solicitude for the baby had become a little disturbed over the way the medical nurse was caring for her. One day when the baby's condition seemed more serious than usual, Mrs. Glover happened to come into the room and Mother asked her advice. Instead of trying to take matters in her own hands or urging Mother to interfere, Mrs. Glover simply spoke quietly and gently to Mother and after that everything was all right.

Mrs. Glover enjoyed talking with my father, when he came to spend the weekends on this visit to the Nashes, and they used to have some good laughs together. Father was full of all kinds of interesting stories and amusing anecdotes. Mrs. Glover often stayed at the table after the meal was over, listening with interest to what he and the other members of the family had to say, joining freely in the conversation herself. I used to look forward to these hospitable occasions, for we all had such a happy time together.

I remember that Mrs. Glover had a huge, solid-silver napkin ring that someone had presented to her. One time while at the table she was telling Father about it, and handed it to him to look at. As they arose from the table, he unconsciously slipped it into his pocket and they stood together for a few moments deep in conversation. Just as Mrs. Glover was about to leave the room, Father happened to put his hand in his pocket and there was the napkin ring. He pulled it out and returned it, Mrs. Glover laughing about it as if she thought it a good joke. I remember Father saying, after she had left the room, "What would she have thought if I had gone home with it?"

Mrs. Glover thought a great deal of my mother and I know she hoped she would become one of her students. She told Mother she was a natural Christian Scientist and asked her to go through class with her. This was while we were making our first visit at No. 8 Broad Street. Somehow the idea did not appeal to Mother then and she declined. Thinking, I suppose, that Mother might have refused because of the money involved, Mrs. Glover offered to give her class instruction free of charge, telling Mother, "You will be such a wonderful help." But still Mother could not understand how she could be of any use to Mrs. Glover and did not see that there was any special reason why she should study Christian Science—so the opportunity slipped by.

After I became interested in Christian Science myself and looked back on those earlier days, which Mother and I often used to talk about, it seemed to me that Mrs. Glover probably was not only impressed by Mother's friendly devotion, but by her patience, courage, and unusual insight—qualities our Leader so sorely needed among her workers in those days.

When Mother returned home after this visit with her nephew, the first thing she did was to tell Asa Eddy about her remarkable experience in Lynn. She told him she had met "the most wonderful woman that ever was," and that if he would go to her she was sure he could be healed. She said that Mrs. Glover held classes where she taught people how to heal and advised him to go to her at once and study with her. He was extremely interested and told Mother he would surely follow her advice.

Whether he went immediately to Mrs. Glover after that talk I never knew. But I do know that Mother, who was now a frequent caller at Mrs. Glover's, told Mrs. Glover that she was sending a friend to her who was in urgent need of healing, and who could be of great help to her. And she informed her of all she knew about Asa Eddy. Some time after Mrs. Glover married Asa Eddy she wrote to Mother saying that she could never repay the debt she owed her for sending Mr. Eddy to her, because he had proved such a blessing and help. I know this made Mother very happy. Not being able to see how she could be of any use to Mrs. Glover herself, she welcomed the news that her friend had proved so valuable an assistant.

After he married Mrs. Glover, Asa Eddy still continued to visit us, though not so frequently. I remember these later visits quite well, for my aunt, Mrs. Nancy Benson, who had occupied part of our large house in East Boston, was quite disgusted when my mother became so friendly with Mrs. Glover. She had met Asa Eddy at our home and liked him very much, but when she learned that he was investigating Christian Science and had married "that woman," as she called her then, she had no use for him and would have nothing to do with him. She said it was nothing but witchcraft—and I suppose it did seem like that to many good people in those days. Years later my aunt became interested in Christian Science herself, through my husband's experience, and after that she always felt kindly toward Mrs. Eddy.

By the time Mrs. Glover married Mr. Eddy she was becoming so busy that Mother did not feel it was right to go to see her too much. She had been in the habit of going to her whenever there was anything she wanted to talk over and she wrote to her freely. Whenever she had needed help for any physical ailment she had called upon Mrs. Glover, for she did not then believe that other Christian Scientists could heal. After Mrs. Eddy withdrew from the practice, Mother got along as best she could, reading the First Edition of *Science and Health* which Mrs. Glover had given her before she married.

The glamour of Mrs. Eddy's personality seemed to be all that we wanted then. I do not think it occurred to Mother that this textbook was something to be studied. But, of course, Mother had had actual proof that its author could heal, and she never had had proof that her students could or that the study of the book would do this. Possibly that may have accounted for her feeling as she did.

It was only a few months after our stay with my cousins, early the following winter, that I had an attack of membranous croup. I had suffered with this all during childhood, and Father and Mother both used to become very fearful that they would lose me during one of these attacks. But this time Mother was so sure that Mrs. Glover could heal me that she wrapped me up in a blanket and started off to Lynn in a heavy snowstorm, my Aunt Nancy accompanying us to the station.

Aunt Nancy kept telling Mother that she was crazy to take me on such a journey a day like that and I would surely die. But Mother went right on and finally got me to Lynn. When she reached Mrs. Glover's house, she went straight to the back door so that she could get in more quickly. Mrs. Glover came to the door at once and, as calmly as if nothing was the matter, said that if I would run upstairs and play I would be all right. I do not remember much about it, except that I did as she told me, for I had been taught to be obedient. I ran upstairs to the Nashes' apartment and immediately I was all right. That was the end of this awful condition.

We stayed at the house all night and in the morning Father came over after us. Mrs. Glover saw Father then and told him that it was his fault that I had had these spells. I remember being very much distressed when I heard her say that, for I thought Father was just about perfect—he had always been so good to me. Of course, I did not then understand what she meant and possibly Father did not altogether. But Mrs. Glover knew that I was the only surviving child in our family, my two brothers having passed on in infancy, and that Father felt a special solicitude for me, fearing and worrying in such a way as to anticipate these terrible attacks long before there was any sign of them. That no doubt was what she was trying to point out to him, so that he would protect me from such thoughts. Father was so delighted that I was healed that I do not believe he would have minded anything Mrs. Glover might have said and I am sure in his way he tried to follow out her instructions.

Anyhow, Father had gained such confidence in Mrs. Glover's healing ability that, though he was not able to see the need of studying Christian Science himself, being a naturally happy and healthy man, he was not afraid to trust his family to her and never hesitated to send others to Mrs. Glover if they seemed in need.

A carpenter came to our house, for some reason, who had his arm in a sling. Father asked him what the trouble was and he said that he had strained the ligaments and paralysis had set in. The arm was partly withered and all the physicians said that it would continue to wither. He said that he had been to the best physicians and hospitals there were. Father told him about Mrs. Eddy and asked him if he went to her to come and tell him the result. About a week later the carpenter came to the house to tell Father that he was completely healed.

I might add that when this man came to see Mrs. Glover she was too busy to come down to talk with him and just opened a window in her parlor room on the second floor and called down to him. Father never told me any details of this experience other than those I have related, but as far as I know this was the only conversation Mrs. Glover had with the man and he came away healed.

Mother's confidence had remained unshaken from the very first, and she continued to give expression to that confidence by sending her friends and acquaintances to Mrs. Eddy for help.

As I recall the Broad Street house in those days when we visited there, Mrs. Glover's classroom was on the ground floor. I distinctly remember Mother telling me that I must never go in there and I never did. At the time we stayed with my cousins they lived on the second floor. The kitchen in the rear to the right was used as a dining room. There were a large range and a big dining table in the kitchen, besides other furniture necessary for the double purpose to which the room was put. In looking over the house more recently I noticed that the kitchen seemed very small—too small to hold all the things that were in it those earlier years. It is possible that changes were made in the interior by later tenants.

At the time we visited there, there was no hallway connecting the rooms on this floor, each room opening into the other. Adjoining the kitchen on the right was a sleeping room which my cousins used, and next to this on the same side of the house was an extra room which Mother and I used when we visited there. On the left side of the house in the rear was the dining room which my cousins used as their living room.

Next to this was a good-sized front room which was reserved for Mrs. Glover as her parlor. One day my cousin took me to the door and opened it just enough to let me peek in. The room contained all kinds of things, presents he said that Mrs. Glover's students had given her. Mrs. Glover also took me in there once and showed me the things in the room.

There was a balcony on the second floor just back of the room used as a living room. It was quite small and I think was reached by a window. Morning glories and moonflowers that had been trained on long strings grew up the side of the balcony and formed a regular screen. There were boxes along the railing filled with flowers, and there were stacks of calla lilies. Mrs. Glover used this balcony as a sort of refuge where she could get away by herself, though I do not think she ever spent a great deal of time there.

I used to be permitted to go out on this balcony with my dolls to play, for the yard was small and I was not allowed there. Mrs. Glover occasionally took me on the balcony with her and then I thought I was just about in heaven.

It seemed so wonderful to be in this pretty place with such a beautiful lady. While I played, she would talk with me, and sometimes sit down for a few minutes, taking me in her lap. How I used to love to cuddle up to her as she rocked back and forth. She was always so gentle and sweet with me that I know she must have loved little children.

Sometimes she took me up to her room in the attic. It was located toward the rear of the third floor and lighted by a single skylight. It was here that she did all her writing. I remember being filled with awe and secret delight at being taken up there where she never allowed anyone to come. I do not recall much about that room now, save that it was small and had, as I then thought, a funny little window in the roof.

There was a small haircloth rocker in which Mrs. Glover always sat—the same rocker that stood in the elevator at Chestnut Hill and has since been removed to the Lynn house and restored to its original place in the attic room. Many is the time that Mrs. Glover took me in her arms, or let me climb up in her lap, and rocked me in that chair. I was small for my age, and though she was not a robust woman, it never seemed to tire her to have me play around or sit on her lap.

Years later, when The Mother Church had been dedicated and the Mother's Room* was open to the public, I went to see it with other visitors. When the door opened, there at my left was a large picture of that same haircloth rocker. I was so astonished that

---

*Mother's Room was a small apartment built in the Original Mother Church for Mrs. Eddy's use during visits to Boston. "Mother" was an endearing term for Mrs. Eddy used by many early followers. In 1903 she requested that she no longer be called "Mother," and in 1908 announced that the Mother's Room was closed to visitors. (See *Church Manual* by Mary Baker Eddy, pp. 64 and 69.)

without realizing what I was saying I burst out, "Why there's the very chair I rocked in." When I realized what I had done I felt terribly—it was as if I had advertised myself to everybody there, and that was the last thing in the world I wanted to do. I never spoke that way again.

In my early childhood, when we first lived in Chelsea, I had a playhouse. It was put upstairs when we moved into the house and over it hung a large picture of Mrs. Glover (it looked like an enlargement of a steel engraving), which she had given to Mother just before she married Asa Eddy. Mother spent so much time downstairs that I did not like to be left alone and so my playhouse was moved down to the dining room, but the picture remained upstairs.

I was very happy to be near my mother until I discovered that the picture of the beautiful lady was missing; then I insisted that there be another one to hang above my playhouse. Childlike, when I accompanied Mother on one of her calls on Mrs. Glover, I told Mrs. Glover that I wanted her picture to hang in the dining room. It was not long before she sent us a duplicate of the one we had, which I always called "my picture." Every morning when I came downstairs I always said, "Good morning," to it. This picture did not show Mrs. Glover with long curls. In fact, I do not recall ever having seen Mrs. Glover with her hair in curls. Her hair was always piled up on her head. She had a round pretty figure in those days and always wore plain dark clothes.

Mrs. Glover had given Mother a copy of the First Edition of *Science and Health,* and after that she gave her each edition as it was published, writing some appropriate inscription on the flyleaf. When she gave these to her, she suggested that it would be a help if Mother would share whatever she knew about Christian Science with others and lend the book to anyone who expressed a wish for it. In accordance with Mrs. Glover's request, Mother was very generous in sharing her copies of the textbook with her friends and acquaintances. Whenever she met someone who was interested or who was in need, she would recommend

Mrs. Eddy's book and then kindly lend one of her own copies. The result was that some of the books became badly defaced and others were lost. As the years went by and Mother could not get her books back, she felt very badly about it, for she had cherished them as gifts from Mrs. Eddy and had expected to keep them.

By late summer 1879 Mrs. Eddy had organized her Church. I do not recall that either Father or Mother attended any of these very early meetings, for they were not interested in Christian Science as a religion. The friendship for its Founder continued, however, and as a result I was frequently twitted by the children in school and got quite used to having people think my parents were queer because they liked Mrs. Eddy.

Despite public misrepresentation and the fact that Mrs. Eddy was becoming so busy that Mother only saw her occasionally, Mother never lost her love and respect for her. The more she was maligned the more Mother defended her. Mother always said she was a good, wonderful, beautiful woman.

Even when Mrs. Eddy removed to Boston, Mother did not lose track of her, but went to call on her occasionally at Columbus Avenue and also at Commonwealth Avenue. When Mother went to call on her she would say to come oftener, that, although she was a busy woman, she would always see her when she came. Mother, however, did not go very often, knowing that Mrs. Eddy was so busy. She took me with her on two of these visits to the Metaphysical College and once to Commonwealth Avenue, but I do not remember anything about them now. I think Mother thought it was asking a great deal of Mrs. Eddy for us both to come and that is why she did not bring me with her more often.

During 1887–1888 Mrs. Eddy's son George Glover came East and made his home in Chelsea for a while. I remember the first time I saw him he was standing with his back to me in the door-way of the grocery store, not far from our home, where we traded. I did not know who he was then, but I recall very vividly how surprised I was to see a man of such peculiar appearance. He stood there calling out his orders in a loud voice, and his manner was so boisterous and his costume so unusual that I could not help telling my mother about it when I returned home.

I do not recollect the details of his clothes now, except that his legs were encased in great high boots such as I had never seen before, and his trousers were tucked into these boots. I remember his hair was long and he wore a beard. He seemed entirely out of keeping with the surroundings there.

When Mother heard he was in town she was anxious to meet him, and knowing that he was Mrs. Eddy's son, I am sure she wished to befriend him. But when she finally did meet him and talked with him in this same grocery store, a short while after I first saw him, she came away disappointed and convinced that they had nothing in common. Whether she ever told Mrs. Eddy about this meeting, or Mrs. Eddy ever talked with her about George Glover, I do not know.

Late in 1888 Mother went to see Mrs. Eddy at Commonwealth Avenue just after she had adopted Dr. E. J. Foster. She did not take me with her this time but I well remember her telling Father and me about it. She was so concerned when she learned what Mrs. Eddy had done that she went right over to see her and told her she wanted to meet this adopted son. Mrs. Eddy called him in and after having a few pleasant words with them he left. Mother was a very intuitive person, and she read Dr. Foster so thoroughly in those few minutes that she was convinced he was not the right person to be with a friend so dear to her as Mrs. Eddy, and frankly told her so. Mrs. Eddy listened patiently without making any comments, except to try to assure Mother that everything would be all right. Mother came home and sputtered so much about it, feeling so sure that her best friend was getting the worst of the bargain, that Father had to tell her to stop talking about it.

In 1889, just before Mrs. Eddy left Boston to make her home in Concord, Mother had another visit with her. Mrs. Eddy was glad to see her—she was always generous in sharing her time with Mother—and told her that she hoped she would visit her in Concord. Mother never did so, however, as she felt that Mrs. Eddy's own students had the prior right.

Though Mother was an ardent Universalist, she used to go to Boston occasionally to hear Mrs. Eddy preach. She took me with her a few times, but I do not recall anything at all about the services. I was in my teens then and intensely interested in music, which I was teaching at the time. So when I went to the services in Chickering Hall my attention was more occupied by Mrs. Eddy as a beautiful woman and family friend, rather than as a preacher and pastor.

During the years of Mrs. Eddy's acquaintance with my mother she had kept in touch with her through correspondence. I remember that after Mother passed on, somewhere around 1899, I had to go through her effects and found a great pile of letters all in Mrs. Eddy's handwriting, dating back to the very beginning of their friendship together in Lynn. They had all been carefully sorted and arranged in chronological order in a cabinet desk. They filled all one side of a drawer which was probably about twenty-four inches deep. But they were completely destroyed in the Chelsea fire of 1908 and I never knew exactly what their contents were.

When I finally married Mr. Danforth P. W. Parker, Jr., in 1892, it seemed to me that my cup of happiness was full. What more could one ask? I had a wonderful father and mother, who had taught me to make light of sickness and to look on the bright side of things, and who had always been kind and generous to me; a husband who was one of the finest men who ever lived; a dear little home of my own and my music.

After two years of all this happiness my husband came down with pneumonia, and though under the physician's care he pulled through, he did not seem to recover from the ill effects and nothing he could do seemed to really heal him. Then it was that Christian Science was presented to us through *The Christian Science Journal,* a magazine which neither of us had seen or heard of before. We were visiting my husband's mother at the time, who had a home in Barnstable, Massachusetts. Mr. and Mrs. Albert F. Conant* lived right next door, and I remember one day while my husband and I were sitting on the veranda that Bert Conant (as we called him) passed the house with his arms full of papers. I asked him what he was carrying and he replied, *Christian Science Journals.* When I questioned him further he told us more about the *Journal* and mentioned Mrs. Eddy's name. This started a long conversation between us and ended in Mr. Conant's advising my husband to try Christian Science.

I have always felt that the *Journal* was the means of first awakening me to the value of Christian Science, and it certainly was what Mr. Conant told us about it that time that prompted my husband's interest. When I told my mother of this talk with Mr. Conant, she gave us one of her old copies of *Science and Health,* which my husband immediately began to read. As this early edition did not seem adequate, we purchased the latest one and then Mr. Parker asked for Christian Science treatment. He was greatly helped and became convinced that Christian Science was the religion for him.

I was teaching Sunday School in the Church of the Redeemer in Chelsea (the Universalist church of which we were members and which my parents attended) at the time. Mr. Parker was the youngest deacon who had ever been appointed to that office and was an earnest and faithful worker. Now, however, that he was becoming interested in Christian Science we went to The Mother Church in addition to attending our own services. Though, I must confess, we did not at first understand what it was all about, we could not help but feel the wonderfully harmonious atmosphere. My husband's growing perception of divine Principle made him realize that I was looking to Mrs. Eddy's personality more than to the truths embodied in her religion, but he was very

*Albert F. Conant was compiler of the Concordances to Mrs. Eddy's writings and organist in The Mother Church for fifteen years. Mrs. Conant was Second Reader of The Mother Church at the time the Extension was dedicated in 1906.

patient and made no attempt to influence me. He knew I would awaken and turn to Principle in my own way.

When my husband finally decided to break away from the Universalist church, I was quite shocked. I remember it was Communion Sunday and much to my surprise he refused to go to church with me. He said very quietly, but with a conviction I could not mistake, "I shall never go to another Communion. If we always have Christ with us, why go to Communion?" I could not understand him at all and replied that I would never leave my church, no matter what anyone else did. Of course, when his fellow members found out that Mr. Parker intended to leave his church, they did everything they could to discourage him. He had been a splendid worker and naturally they did not want to lose him. The pastor tried to encourage him to stay, but I remember he was very kindly about it and made no effort to persuade him against his will.

As I began to see how strong my husband's convictions were, I wondered whether there might not really be something in Christian Science as a religion after all. I did not like to go my own way alone, for my husband and I were close companions, and I wanted to help him, so I began to investigate a little myself in an effort to see something beyond the personality of its Leader. It took me a long time to do this and I went through all sorts of phases of self-condemnation and uncertainty. Not until 1901 did I really feel ready to leave my old church and become a Christian Scientist. In November of that year my husband and I both became members of The Mother Church. By that time I realized how much Christian Science had helped us and could understand in some little way what a truly great religion it was.

At the time we became members of The Mother Church, I remember that Mr. William Johnson, who was then Clerk, told us that our letter of recommendation was one of the most beautiful he had ever read. Our former pastor, Rev. R. Perry Bush, had a wide reputation for his liberality and I do not think he ever entertained a single unkind thought about Christian Science or its Leader.

As I look back on all those early years, it is a mystery to me that my active interest in Christian Science was delayed so long. Not only had I known Mrs. Eddy, been healed myself and seen my mother and others healed and comforted, but I had seen my husband helped and been closely enough associated with the activities of the Cause, through The Christian Science Publishing Society, to know that it was something to be reckoned with.

It was in the early fall of 1898 that I was called to serve the Publishing Society. I remember receiving a telegram late one night, saying that I was wanted at Mr. Joseph Armstrong's office the next day. I had no idea why I had been sent for, but as I knew Mr. Armstrong very well, I did not hesitate to answer the call. Mr. Armstrong knew all about my early acquaintance with Mrs. Eddy, for my family had met him frequently at the Conant house on the Cape, and he had questioned me about my childhood with a great deal of interest.

When I came to Boston the next morning, I went straight to Mr. Armstrong's office on the first floor of No. 95 Falmouth Street. He told me right off that he wanted me to come and help out on the new *Christian Science Weekly.** I was greatly surprised. Though I had had some valuable business experience in the offices of the American Express Company, it did not occur to me that opportunity might arise for me to make further use of it. Then, too, it was not necessary for me to work at that time, as I already had my music; and my husband, who was not strong, needed some care, and there was our home to look after. I felt my place was there and told Mr. Armstrong so.

Knowing my devotion to Mrs. Eddy, it did not take him long to put my excuses aside and say the right thing, for his next

*The *Christian Science Weekly,* first published in September 1898, was renamed the *Christian Science Sentinel* in January 1899.

words were, "But she needs you." That put a different light on the matter. To work for the Publishing Society was something that I did not care particularly about doing then, but to work there because Mrs. Eddy wanted me to was quite another thing. But even then I felt that I should first tell my family and see what they had to say before coming to any decision. Mr. Armstrong tried to make me see that they needed me right away and to persuade me to start in that very morning, but I insisted that I must go home first.

My husband was having Christian Science treatment at the time and was becoming an earnest student. When I got home and told him about my experience, he was quite ashamed of me and said that I should have stayed as I was asked to. This did not satisfy me, however, and I went over to talk to Mother. She was ill then and needed my care, so I was sure she would not want me to go. When I told her about it all and repeated what Mr. Armstrong had said about Mrs. Eddy wanting me to come to the Publishing Society offices to work, she replied, "Of course, if she wants it, that is the thing to do." "But shouldn't I stay home and take care of you?" I questioned. "If you can go there you will be filled with good thoughts and that will help me more than if you stayed here and got full of sick thoughts," was my mother's prompt reply.

There seemed to be nothing else for me to do, so I changed my clothes and prepared to return to the Publishing House and start right in as Mr. Armstrong had asked me to that very day. I did not think at the time that I would stay long—probably a few days or weeks at the most—but that work has continued in one form or another from that day to this.

The Publishing House occupied the two brick dwellings at Nos. 95–97 Falmouth Street at that time. You entered by way of No. 95 directly into a reception room. In the corner at the right of the entrance door was a mantel over a fireplace and here the flowers, which had been used in The Mother Church, were always kept. Fresh flowers were put in the Mother's Room and after they had lost their first freshness Mr. Armstrong used to bring them over and place them on this mantel. The furnishings in this room, as in the other rooms in the Publishing House, were of the plainest, simplest kind.

We had our hands full those days, more than we could possibly do. In fact, we never went home without leaving a lot of work undone—it just seemed as if we were never able to catch up. Our day commenced at eight in the morning, as I remember, and continued until five-thirty, including Saturdays and holidays, and often we came back after supper and worked until late at night wrapping *Sentinels*. I know there were times when I did not get home until twelve or one o'clock at night. It was not always very comfortable working either, especially on the third floor during the summer. We had no electric fan then and sometimes it became unbearably warm up there. As I remember we had no telephone on the third floor either.

All during those early years with the Publishing Society my interest in Mrs. Eddy was changing and assuming a different aspect. I saw her not only as a lovely woman but began to recognize her as the Leader of a great Cause. I never heard from her personally then, except once, when she sent a message to me asking for the address of my cousins, the Nashes, who had lived with her in Lynn. The one who brought this message to me said that Mrs. Eddy wished me to know how glad she was that I was working for the Publishing Society. Unfortunately, I was not able to furnish Mrs. Eddy with the information she desired. I never knew what Mrs. Eddy's reason was for asking me this, as she did not communicate with me further on the subject, and the few times I then saw her were in public where I never had opportunity to speak with her.

In 1899, when we learned in the office that Mrs. Eddy was to come down to Boston to address the Annual Meeting of The Mother Church in Tremont Temple, we were all very much excited. Miss Maude Wright, who worked in the room with me, had never seen Mrs. Eddy and I, too, was eager to get a fresh

Mrs. Eddy at State Fair, Concord, New Hampshire, 1901

glimpse of her. Neither of us was a member of The Mother Church and we did not see how it could be managed. Mr. Nunn was then in the Publishing House and was to be on the platform at Tremont Temple with Mrs. Eddy. When Miss Wright and I told him how anxious we were to see Mrs. Eddy, he said that, if we went down and stood on the street near the main entrance of Tremont Temple, he thought we might be able to see her as she left the carriage.

There was a holiday air of anticipation in the whole office that day, and when we closed for the afternoon all the Church members, of course, went to the meeting, while Miss Wright and I made our way to Tremont Temple and edged up close to the entrance. After we had been standing on the street for some time, a hack drove up and Mrs. Eddy alighted and walked into the building as daintily and spryly as if she had been a young woman. Miss Wright and I were so thrilled that we waited in the hope we might see Mrs. Eddy leave. In a short time she reappeared and drove off in her carriage. We were both so up in the seventh heaven that I do not believe either of us could have described her—we just knew that we had received some wonderful, beautiful impression that was indefinable.

In 1901 Mr. Parker and I went up to Concord to the State Fair. Mr. Parker had never seen Mrs. Eddy before, and I remember how happy he was when her carriage stopped just in front of us, so close that we could have reached out our hands and touched her. She was leaving the fairgrounds and there was such a jam at the entrance that it took some time for her carriage to drive through, but she sat there quite unperturbed, bowing and smiling to everyone.

After I became a member of The Mother Church my husband and I visited Pleasant View in 1903, when Mrs. Eddy welcomed her followers from the balcony. We stood right under the balcony where we could see her plainly and hear every word she said. After she had finished speaking, I felt as if I wanted to go off quietly by myself and just think about it.

I also visited Concord when the Concord church was dedicated, but only had opportunity to see Mrs. Eddy as she passed by in her carriage.

In these later years she did not look as I remembered her in Lynn. In the Lynn days women's styles were more severe and everyone wore dark tight-fitting bodices with long full skirts. I always remember her with dark hair dressed in waves close to her head, with never a hair out of place; smooth, close-fitting dark dresses, very plain except for a little passementerie or lace about the throat and wrists, and little if any jewelry. In later years, as her hair became white, her face thinner and figure more slender, the styles changed radically—fluffy, ruffled, light-colored clothes became the fashion, thin silks and softer satins replacing the more austere heavy velvets and stiff taffetas. These clothes made a great difference in her appearance; the airiness of silks, chiffons, and laces and pastel effects of color provided just the right background for her spirituelle loveliness.

Not long after our visit to Pleasant View in 1903 my husband passed on (January 1904), leaving my father and me alone in the house together. Though my father was not actively interested in Christian Science himself, he used to enjoy attending the services with me occasionally. It was on a Sunday morning in April 1908, while we were attending services in First Church, Chelsea, together, that the terrible Chelsea fire broke out and raged with such disastrous results.

Our home was right in the path of the fire in the center of the city and was totally destroyed. We were unable to save anything. All the letters Mrs. Eddy had written to my mother, the books she had given us and her pictures were reduced to ashes. Therefore, today I have no evidence of those dear childhood associations and my mother's friendship with this great woman save my happy memories. Fortunately, my memory has been very reliable, so that I have not had much difficulty in recalling these early experiences, except, of course, that many of the details have slipped away and the dates, of which I have little record, are sometimes hard to recall accurately.

I have never been in the habit of talking much about those days, so that the memory of them has lain dormant for a long while. The only time I had occasion to refer to them was when Mr. Alfred Farlow asked me to let Sibyl Wilbur O'Brien interview me, sometime in 1906 or 1907, I believe. I was very reluctant to do this and only consented after Mr. Farlow said that Mrs. Eddy wanted me to. My father and I then went to see Miss Wilbur on Blagden Street, near the Boston Public Library. I related my story to her, but she did not take any notes of what I said, remarking that her memory would be sufficient.

Miss Wilbur told Father and me that when she was sent out on her first interview to Pleasant View and got on the train, she insisted to herself that no matter what she found out during her visit to Concord she would tell the truth about it. She said that as she drew near her destination she became very miserable and wished she had not come; she did not know what to expect or what to ask. She had heard many rumors, but beyond that knew nothing about Mrs. Eddy. She told us that when she reached Pleasant View she was ushered into the reception room downstairs and felt that she never could bring herself to go to Mrs. Eddy's rooms to talk with her.

[On Miss Wilbur's calling again the next day] someone announced that she could come up, and she said that when she reached the top stair she saw a slight little woman standing on the opposite side of the room looking out the window, with her hands crossed in back of her. It was Mrs. Eddy.

Miss Wilbur said that, when she looked at Mrs. Eddy, it was like a revelation and she realized how everyone had misunderstood her. Miss Wilbur did not tell us anything about the interview, but said that when she returned to Boston she wanted to see The Mother Church Extension, which was then under construction. [Some time] later she entered the auditorium and saw the words "To-day the healing power of Truth is widely demonstrated as an immanent, eternal Science." She said she was so impressed by the significance of the word "to-day" that she was convinced Mrs. Eddy had the truth. She wrote her article, but the paper for which she had written it would not print it as she wanted it, so she arranged with *Human Life* magazine to take it. This, I understand, was the beginning of her book about Mrs. Eddy.

During all this time I had been continuing my work with the Publishing Society which had been growing by leaps and bounds. We had now outgrown the houses on Falmouth Street, which had to be torn down to make way for The Mother Church Extension, and that year moved to Huntington Avenue.

While we were getting the building ready at 107 Falmouth Street, Mrs. Eddy was living at Chestnut Hill. During those years it was my good fortune to see her in her carriage a few times when she was taking her daily drive. I had a cousin, Lewis Maynell, living in Chestnut Hill on Commonwealth Avenue not far from Mrs. Eddy's home, whom I visited quite frequently. One time, when I was on my way up the hill to his home, Mrs. Eddy drove down the hill and stopped right near me. It looked as though she had stopped to take in the view. She did not glance in my direction, and I do not know whether she would have recognized me if she had, it was so many years since she had seen me. But I was delighted to have had a glimpse of her anyway, and when I got to my cousin's home told him so. He replied in a matter-of-fact voice, "Why I see her every day. What of it?" Not being interested in Christian Science, of course, he had no idea what it meant to me.

This same cousin was a well-known artist. While Mrs. Eddy was residing at Chestnut Hill, he was doing a bas-relief of Chief Justice Fuller and of President Theodore Roosevelt. He was very anxious to paint Mrs. Eddy's portrait, feeling that she would be a fine subject. He asked me for a picture of her and I brought him an 1886 edition of *Science and Health* which had her picture as the frontispiece. He liked the picture, and remarked that he wanted to do a picture himself when he could get to it, but that it would be absolutely necessary for him to see Mrs. Eddy for a sitting. He never did see Mrs. Eddy for this purpose and the portrait was never painted.

Not long after this Mrs. Eddy passed on, and despite the fact that she had not seen and talked with me for years, I felt as though I had lost a dear personal friend. The thought of all the beautiful tenderness and love shown me in my childhood and the staunch friendliness she had so freely given to my mother had remained with me. And while as a child and young girl I had taken it all for granted, as I grew to womanhood and became interested in Christian Science, I saw that Mother and I had shared in a rare privilege.

I have always been so grateful that I did finally turn to Christian Science and thus have had opportunity to see Mrs. Eddy in the right light as the Discoverer and Founder of this wonderful [Science of] Christ, Truth. I realize more and more that everything worthwhile in my experience—my friends, the work in The Christian Science Publishing Society in which I have been so happy all these years, my joy and peace of mind—is due to the divine Science which this grand woman labored so patiently to give to the world. And I am grateful beyond words that the study of this Science has enabled me in some measure to turn from personality to Principle in accordance with her teachings.

A Worker in the Massachusetts Metaphysical College

JULIA S. BARTLETT

We were left six fatherless and motherless children. I, the eldest, was sixteen years of age, while the youngest was but a babe of three years, a delicate little girl who needed much a mother's care and love, as did all.

I would pass lightly over the few years of my young life that followed, and the change that came so suddenly from loving care to cold and heartless treatment. We were able to make remuneration for all that was done for us, but that seemingly made no difference. The sad, little faces told the story of the hardships that were endured, and while my heart ached for the little ones more than for myself, I was powerless to save them from it.

All this experience was not lost on me, and I am very grateful that the time came that I could forgive and forget all the hardships of the past and love sincerely those through whom they came while they returned it in full measure. Who will say that this experience was not just what was needed to learn this great lesson?

These first great trials were the means of turning my thought more to spiritual things, and although I was like a child groping in the dark, there was always a glimmer of light that brightened my path and sustained, comforted, and cheered me. I felt God was caring for me in ways I knew not and when the way seemed hard it was God's will and all for my good. Oh, how little I knew what God is and that it is not His will that any should suffer. These experiences during my schooldays probably

28

served to develop and strengthen my character and make me more thoughtful and earnest in every line of action.

I loved to go sometimes with my dearest school friend to some beautiful spot where we would be by ourselves, and there we would talk of spiritual things and wonder what was truth and what was not, always looking forward to a future world happiness, not knowing it was a present possibility.

I found that to be converted according to my orthodox belief brought no lasting peace or happiness and that I was the same girl as before, with the same faults and failings still with me. I had not learned that I must work out my own salvation as the Scriptures command and that our great Master taught the way which must be *understood* instead of merely believed.

As time went on and I was beyond the schooldays, my thought continued to open to the truth sufficiently to drop some of my old theological views, and when my friends inquired as to my creed, I told them I did not think I had any. I felt there was a truth beyond what I knew or had been able to find, and more and more there was a longing and reaching out for it, trying to find it. Many times a day the thought would come, "What is Truth?" until it was the one great question in my mind which I was unable to solve. I then thought "I can only live the best life I know how and trust," but that did not satisfy. I must see my way, have something to hold to and to rest upon. While this evolution was going on in my mind I was not made sad or gloomy thereby, but on the contrary was cheerful and hopeful.

At this stage of experience I was taken very ill and at different times my life was despaired of by physicians, and friends sent for expecting it to be the last time. The case was one of great suffering to human sense and when I saw it lengthening into months and years, I resolved to do my best under the condition in which I was placed that those years of my life might be profitable and no unnecessary burden to others.

Completely shut out from the world for five years, helpless on my bed, weakened by suffering, I could still be patient and cheerful and not a complaining invalid. I made it a point not to talk disease nor wear a long face, but to have a smile for everyone. The physicians remarked that they seldom saw a patient bear suffering with so great fortitude and that mine was the most cheerful sick-room they entered. It was God's dear love that was sustaining and fitting me for the truth that was soon to come, although I knew it not. Twice I was removed on my bed to different cities to be treated by other physicians. All were most interested and kind, and I appreciated their efforts, but material remedies could not heal me.

After seven years there was improvement, but no hopes were given of a final recovery and the remedies used were having no effect. Then I told my friends I was waiting to find something besides material remedies that would heal, when one day a letter came from a friend telling the first I had ever heard of Christian Science. This was in April 1880, when the Science was little known. She also sent a little circular giving account of the first Christian Science Church which was organized with a member-ship of twenty-six and the charter of which was obtained in August 1879, the preceding year. On reading the circular which [described] "a Church designed to perpetuate the teachings of Jesus, to reinstate primitive Christianity, and to restore its lost element of healing," I was much interested, and considering the letter which said this healing was done through Mind, I said I saw no reason why the sick should not be healed in this way.

I asked my friend to recommend a practitioner to take my case, and at the same time I sent for the book, *Science and Health.* She went to Mrs. Eddy for advice, and she put me under the care of her husband, Dr. Asa G. Eddy. I began to improve immediately and was getting my freedom. I felt like one let out of prison. The fetters of material beliefs and laws were giving way to the higher law of Spirit and the sufferings were correspondingly disappear-ing. I never could describe the sense of freedom that came with a glimpse of this glorious truth. The world was another world to me. All things were seen from a different viewpoint and there was a halo of beauty over all.

I never had seen a Christian Scientist, but my one desire above all others was to see and know the one through whom all this great good had come to the world and to be taught the truth by her, that I might help others. This came about in due time. In about four months from the time I first heard of Christian Science I applied to Mrs. Eddy for class instruction and was accepted.

She made an appointment with me at her home in Lynn, and when I went there, her husband, Dr. Eddy, waited on me. He said Mrs. Eddy was engaged just then, but would see me soon. She came in almost immediately, however, with her hair (which she was arranging) partly down, and said she would not keep me waiting. I felt her love which always made her thoughtful for others, and was perfectly at ease in her presence. She was beautiful, but rather more slender at this time than at a later period. She made arrangements with me about entering her class, and as I knew she had much to attend to, I made my call short.

I think what most impressed me at this first meeting was her spirituality and the place she occupied in the world, and yet she met me just where I was, so simply and sweetly, mindful even of the little things for my comfort. As I went from her presence, I was thinking of the days when I could go to that little home and listen to her wonderful teachings. This home in Lynn was very simple in all its arrangements, but immaculately neat. They kept no servant at that time, but Dr. Eddy did much to help in every way for the Cause that would otherwise take her time, and attended to business outside. He was always the kind husband and friend and ready helper in all things pertaining to the Cause of Christian Science and our beloved Leader.

My first instructions from Mrs. Eddy began September 30, 1880. This class consisted of only three members. Her classes were all small in those days, but she spoke of how much she enjoyed teaching this little class. Her teachings were a wonderful unfolding of Truth to her students. I can seem to see her now as she sat before us with that heavenly spiritual expression which lighted her whole countenance as she expounded the truth contained in her book, *Science and Health*.

When the class was through, my friend, who first told me of Christian Science and who was also in the class, and I lingered a little and were sitting beside our dear teacher while she was talking to us of mortal mind's hatred of Truth and the evil to be overcome. She mentioned an incident of a person coming to her door armed against her, but he was not able to perform his evil work. We were seeing a little what it meant for her to stand where she did—a representative of Truth before a world of error—the cost of it and the glory of it, but we said in a playful, childlike way that amused and comforted her, "They shall not touch you; *we* will help you." My greatest joy today is that I may have been the means of lightening her burdens somewhat in the years that followed.

The first Christian Science Sunday service I ever attended was at this time and was held in the little parlor at 8 Broad Street, Lynn. There were about twenty people present. Mrs. Eddy preached the sermon which healed a young woman sitting near me of an old chronic trouble which physicians were unable to heal. Her husband, who was present with her, went to Mrs. Eddy the next day to thank her for what had been done for his wife. That was the greatest sermon I ever heard, but few were there to hear it.

After class Mrs. Eddy advised me to go to my home in Connecticut and have a little experience in healing, which I did. During this time I often went to Lynn to attend the meetings of the association and to aid our dear teacher as I could in the work of the Cause, although I was only a beginner.

Early in 1881 she called me to Boston, to establish my work there. I became acquainted with Mrs. Abbie K. Whiting, who had been taught Christian Science by Mrs. Eddy a short time before, and we both thought it would be well to start our work together and went out to engage rooms suitable for that purpose, little knowing the opposition we were about to encounter. We had no difficulty in finding desirable rooms in a good locality and a readiness to receive us until it was learned we were Christian Scientists; then objections were made to taking us. Nothing was known of Christian Science and it was looked upon with suspicion. When refused in one house we would try another and we spent days in this way hoping to find a place in Boston to do our work, but no one would receive us.

Then we went to Charlestown and finally were attracted to a house where we were kindly received by one who granted us all the privileges needed to carry on our work, which included the use of the parlor on Friday evening of every week when we would invite people to come and hear the talks we would give in explanation of Christian Science, what it is, and what it would do for them. The good lady said she would help us in notifying her friends, which she did, and we ourselves were active in doing all we could to reach the people, but with all our efforts none came. I then said, "If they do not come to me, I shall go to them," and dear Mrs. Whiting was ready to join me.

We obtained a good number of the pamphlets *Christian Healing,* which was all there was published on Christian Science at that time aside from *Science and Health,* and with these we started out on our mission, selecting one of the best streets and going from house to house, she on one side and I on the other. This was a bold measure for a timid retiring person, costing many a struggle with self. But that was put aside on meeting the lady of the house who in every instance seemed much interested in what I had to tell of Christian Science and expressed a desire to meet with us and to learn more about it, and a pamphlet was left for each family to read in the meantime.

Although we were happy in knowing good had been done, not one came to us from this work. My friend then decided to go to her home for a little, while I was studying what step to take next. I said in the beginning, "There is a world before me needing the truth. If I fail to get work to do, it will be my own fault and if I do not succeed in my first attempt, I will keep on until I do." I might be tested and proven, but I knew if I did my part and God was with me, there could be no failure.

My next attempt to call attention to Christian Science was to have a sign made and put up in the vestibule with this notice neatly painted in gilt letters:

> Meetings held here for the purpose
> of explaining Christian Science on
> Friday evening of every week at 7:30 p.m.
> All cordially invited.

This attracted much attention and many who passed by stopped to read and apparently wondered what it meant, with the result that the following Friday evening we had an audience of eight curiosity seekers as they themselves confessed, but said they were interested in what was said and would come again and bring their friends with them.

There probably were no happier people in Boston than my friend and I at this first sign of interest. It required much courage and many sacrifices of self before we reaped the fruits of our labors, but the reward came and abundantly until the rooms would not hold the people who wanted to know something of Christian Science and to be healed.

In October 1881, eight students who had allowed error to enter their thought united in writing a disloyal letter of false accusations to their Leader and signed their names to the same. This cruel letter was read at a meeting of the Christian Scientist Association in the presence of Mrs. Eddy. She made no reply, and when the meeting, which was held in her house, was closed, she went to her room and all the students went to their homes with the exception of two. These two [together with Mr. Eddy] remained with their beloved teacher to comfort her in her sorrow and anguish.

I was in Salem at that time and could not attend the meeting, but the next morning on hearing what had transpired I took the first train for Lynn, desiring to be with my dear teacher and to be of some service in her hour of trial. Dr. Eddy admitted me to the house. I found Mrs. Eddy seated by the table and the two students who had spent the night with her sitting near. I quietly took a seat near them as did Dr. Eddy also, and listened to Mrs. Eddy, who was talking with a power such as I had never heard before.

Just before I had entered the room she was sitting with the others and the burden was still heavy upon her, when all at once she rose from her chair, stepped out in the room, her face radiant and with a faraway look as if she was beholding things the eye could not see. She began to talk—her language was somewhat in the style of the Scriptures. The three with her, seeing how it was, caught up their pencils and paper and took down what she said. When she was through speaking and came back to the thought of those about her, they were so moved by what they had seen and heard their eyes were filled with tears and one was kneeling by the couch sobbing.

It was at this point, as Mrs. Eddy sat down and began talking to them, that I arrived. When she was through, she said, "I want you three to stay with me three days." She said she did not know what might be but felt there would be a great deal for us.

Those three days were wonderful. It was as if God was talking to her and she would come to us and tell us the wonderful revelations that came. We were on the mount. We felt that we must take the shoes from off our feet, that we were standing on holy ground. What came to me at that time will never leave me.

November 9, 1881, Mrs. Eddy was ordained pastor of the Church of Christ (Scientist) at 8 Broad Street, Lynn, in her little parlor, with about fifteen present. Mrs. Whiting extended the right hand of fellowship. A table stood in the center of the room and Mrs. Eddy, Mrs. Whiting, and I were on one side while on the other side were the few students standing. Mrs. Eddy stood so meek, with her head bowed and a beautiful spiritual expression on her face, while this recent student [Mrs. Whiting] took her hand and talked to her like one inspired, as she was. It was *very* impressive. Mrs. Eddy had preached *five* years, but was not ordained until the date given above.

It was in that same little house in Lynn that I united with the Church December 25, 1881. Mrs. Eddy was soon to go to Washington for a time to lecture and teach and to do what she could to start the Science in that important city. For this reason she called a meeting of the Church to be held in the evening, to admit me and one other as members, that we might take our place in the church work during her absence.

Mrs. Eddy's household goods were nearly all packed and taken away to be stored while she was gone, as she knew she would not return to Lynn again but would go to Boston. The floors were bare. There were a few chairs, a small writing desk, and a packing box which stood on end, and Mrs. Eddy sat beside it. There were about ten church members to occupy the available seats. Mrs. Eddy read the seventeenth chapter of John, and her parting remarks to us on the event of her leaving the city and her admonitions in regard to the care of the Church and the Cause sank deeply in our hearts. We were saddened at the thought of parting with our beloved teacher, but were brave and courageous in taking up new responsibilities, resolving to be faithful in following her instructions, knowing that God would give us strength according to our needs.

I was one of four appointed by Mrs. Eddy to conduct the Sunday services during her absence. These four were to alternately prepare a sermon and lead the meetings which were held in the private houses of two of the number chosen who had homes of their own, one in Boston, the other in Charlestown. The services, which were simple, were opened by singing a hymn accompanied by the piano; then followed the reading of the Scriptures, silent prayer and the Lord's Prayer, and the sermon; and they closed with a hymn. The little congregation seemed touched by the simplicity and devotion manifested in these meetings and expressed an interest in the words spoken, and some were healed. Our work went on very harmoniously as we tried to be faithful and follow as best we could the tender admonitions of our beloved Leader.

Early in the month of April Mrs. Eddy came to Boston and received a warm welcome from all her students who were rejoiced to have their dear Leader and teacher with them again. She and her husband, Dr. Asa G. Eddy, stopped at the Parker House in Boston until a suitable place could be found for the Massachusetts Metaphysical College which was chartered in 1881.

One day as I was returning from a call on a patient, I could not dismiss the thought that there was a need for me to see Mrs. Eddy. I told Mrs. Whiting, and she said, "If I felt that way, I would go to her by all means." This I did, and when she opened the door to let me in, she said, "You are just the one I want to see," and that she wanted Mrs. W. and myself to go with her to the College. This came as a great surprise and seemed almost too much for me. I felt my unworthiness and replied, "I do not know as I am equal to filling that place." But my desire was to be of the greatest service possible to her and the Cause, so I said I would do the best I could. I felt it was a great privilege, but I also saw there were great responsibilities.

However, I was reassured by her talk with me and when I returned home to Mrs. Whiting, we were both filled with joy to know we could be with our dear teacher and be of such service to her and the Cause of Christian Science. We then made arrangements to discontinue our work in Charlestown. It was in April 1882 that we entered the College with Mrs. Eddy at 569 Columbus Avenue, Boston, and two years later moved to 571.

Mrs. Eddy's time was filled with the great work which lay before her—in teaching, conducting Sunday services, Friday night meetings, writing, receiving callers, and many other duties connected with the Cause, and Dr. Eddy was constantly of assistance to her. Aside from him there were four students with her at the opening of the College—Mr. Hanover P. Smith, Mrs. Whiting, myself, and one other. It was arranged that I should have a large, pleasant room opposite hers where she could call upon me at any time for assistance, and I endeavored to be alert in finding ways and means to help in the progress of the work, and many were the needs that continually unfolded to us.

One day, when having a talk with her concerning the work, she mentioned something that should be done which was of great importance to the Cause, but she said she did not see how we could do any more. I thought a moment, then said, "I think I can do it." I can now see her beautiful face as she looked at me so earnestly and said, "No, I think you are already doing all you can." Her dear love would not let me undertake more, although I would have been so glad to.

There were so many pressing needs and so few to meet them that the moments were precious. There was work to be done at all hours, but it was a great happiness to in any measure lighten the burdens of the one we loved and to be instrumental in laying the foundation of a great work in truth which was to be the saving of the nations.

If I in proportion to my worthiness drank of her cup, I also rejoiced with her in her marvelous triumph over the claims of evil as they appeared, and her wisdom, spiritual discernment, and courage were an inspiration at all times. I could not come into her presence without feeling an uplift and the love and purity of her thought. I have seen students come from her room so softened and chastened and in tears saying they never saw such love. We saw her teachings exemplified in her life and in the love which heals and saves.

Mrs. Eddy soon taught a Primary class and invited Dr. Eddy and me to sit through this, the first Primary class taught in the College. As we had before been taught by her, she said there were questions in our thought which had to be answered before she could proceed with the class. It was all a rich feast for us, for which we were most grateful.

June 3, 1882, Mrs. Eddy's husband, Dr. Asa Gilbert Eddy,

passed on. He, as nearest her, was a target for error, but he met it manfully and courageously, and the last day seemed to be his best. I accompanied him that day on a little horse-car ride which he enjoyed as a pleasant change, but that night he went quietly while sitting in his chair, the two students with him supposing him to be asleep.

This was a sad experience, not only for our beloved Leader, but for all her students who loved Dr. Eddy for his beautiful, strong character, his gentleness and unselfish love. He was always ready to patiently help another with his clear realization of Truth. His calm, gentle, strong thought comforted our dear Leader and was a great help to her in her work for the Cause.

In July Mrs. Eddy went away for a short time with two students. Mrs. Whiting and I remained at the College to attend to whatever must be done for the Cause while Mrs. Eddy was away.

In Mrs. Eddy's parting with her nearest and dearest loved one on earth I saw her wonderful triumph in marking the way for others out of grief and loss of all things earthly, as in her complete reliance on God she rose with a strength and power that was marvelous. This we witnessed on her return home as she went on with the great work of the Cause. No matter what obstacles there were to be met, or the difficulties of the situation, she was equal to whatever came and we marveled at her great wisdom and understanding.

She made known to her students the needs of the hour and the snares and pitfalls that lay in our path in our warfare against error and how to avoid them. Happy was the student who obeyed her instructions, for in obedience to her teachings was his salvation, and through disobedience many lost their way. They were not ready to recognize the error that was blinding them and to yield up their material views, love of self and worldly ambition, and follow the leadings of the divine Mind. This was her experience with many with whom she had labored long and patiently in the early days of Christian Science.

Then there were others who had not been watchful and had

wandered back into their old material thought and ways, until I was the oldest loyal student of Christian Science in the world, and when Mrs. Eddy saw this coming, she said to me, "And will you leave me also?" I replied, "I think if I have been able to stand against what I have so far, I will be able to, whatever comes in the future." She said, *"I think so too."* I have always found God sufficient for all things, and like Paul I would say: "Most gladly therefore will I rather glory in my infirmities, that the power of Christ may rest upon me" (II Cor. 12:9).

Mr. Calvin A. Frye was soon added to the number in the College. He remained our Leader's faithful helper as long as she was personally with us.

September 8, 1882, it was voted to hold Sunday services at the College, where they were held until in November 1883, and then at Hawthorne Hall which seated about two hundred and fifty. As Treasurer of the Church, I often found the subscriptions insufficient to meet the bills. This lack I supplied from time to time from my own purse, in order that the payments might be made promptly and that there be no debts. There were many uses for what we had and not a great abundance to draw from. The great part of my time was given to work that brought no material remuneration.

I took a few patients and had good success in healing, and this supplied me with necessary funds, until all at once not one came to be healed. I understood the cause of this and worked assiduously to overcome the error, in realizing God's government and that He is the source of supply, and in actively doing my part to start my practice again, yet with no apparent result. To be sure I had all I could do with work for the Cause, but my little practice which had met my daily expenses was taken from me. To reduce expenses I then began to take my meals out and to reduce the supply as well, and for the first time I knew what it was to suffer from hunger day after day.

I did not trouble Mrs. Eddy or anyone with the extreme conditions, so far as I could hide them. It was my problem to solve. I finally thought relief must come soon if I was to remain in the College, and taking my Bible for my guidance, I opened to these words: "She . . . shall remain in thine house." It was no longer a question with me. I must and could work it out. Then one day patients began to come. The attempt to take me away and deprive Mrs. Eddy of the help she needed had failed and I had no more trouble that way, and she said I never would.

This experience which was new to me, and my dependence for relief wholly on God, was a most valuable lesson for which I have always been grateful. I remarked to Mrs. Eddy, "We are commanded to take up our cross daily, but I am not doing so, for I do not see any to take up." Her answer was, "It is because it has ceased to be a cross."

We had very happy, restful times together when Mrs. Eddy would sometimes come with us in the parlor after the day's work and we listened to her sweet voice while she sang hymns or some sacred song with Mr. Frye accompanying her on the piano. We had no Christian Science hymns then.

When time would admit, she would sit with us and we would have wonderful heart-to-heart talks. Her conversation gave us much to think of and left its impress on my thought, which has been ever with me. Sometimes she would show us how it would be with us and others when farther advanced in our understanding of Truth. The thoughts she expressed were so beautiful, pure, and good.

Mrs. Eddy would sometimes be amused at our little pleasantries, and we enjoyed seeing her sweet, happy smile at what was said. I can see her now as she looked at this time—her face radiant with that spiritual beauty that never could be put on canvas. Her light brown hair which was naturally curly was arranged becomingly. Her eyes had a wonderful spiritual expression, and she had the fair, delicate complexion of youth with often a pink color in her cheeks, but I have seen all this change to the appearance of an aged woman bearing the burden of the sins of the world which, however, would suddenly disappear as her thought was lifted above it.

Work seemed to be accumulating constantly, and it was marvelous what our Leader accomplished. It was in April of this year (1883) when she started *The Christian Science Journal,* acting as its Editor. She saw the great need of such a publication, but it seemed almost incredible that it could be added to the work already being done.

Nevertheless, she did not falter or delay. She must consider and meet the great problems of the hour as they appeared, fill her place at the Sunday services and Friday night meetings, meet with her students as President of the College Association, receive numerous inquirers for the Science, write a great number of letters, all of which had to be written by hand, and with the many perplexities of the students to be settled—with the needed advice and rebuke to the wayward ones—and many more things to be done, it would seem that half had not been told. She never appeared in haste, but I marveled at the pile of letters she would write or the amount of work she would do in a little time.

Sometimes Mrs. Eddy would dictate letters to me, and one day just at night she came to my room and asked me to write a letter for her. I felt that it was almost impossible for me to do more, but sat down to the table while she dictated the letter. I wrote a few lines, then my pen would go no farther. She sternly rebuked the error, thus enabling me to continue my work until it was done. Then on leaving the room she said, "I did not like to speak to you in that way, but I had to." I was thankful for the love expressed by her and for the help given which continued with me.

I never saw a grander demonstration of Truth than I witnessed as a young student when I saw our Leader stand before one who had for a long time seemed to be held by a very stubborn error. When it did not yield, she gradually rose to a greater and greater power until she seemed a tower of strength, not sparing the error the sharp, cutting rebuke necessary for its destruction, until this woman was free, and she has since been a faithful worker in the Cause of Christian Science.

For a time Mrs. Eddy had the students who were in the College meet with her in the parlor each day for Bible study. She would select a chapter and have us explain each verse in turn giving our best thought of it. Then she would explain farther than we were able to see of ourselves. We looked forward with interest to this instructive, helpful study with her, which was specially needed at that time. It better fitted us to do our part in giving the true meaning of the Scriptures to others when called upon by her when for a short time the Sunday services were changed and Bible lessons were given instead of the regular sermon.

About March 1, 1884, a young woman whom physicians were not able to heal was sent to me for treatment in Christian Science by a physician in New Hampshire who was attending her case. In nine days she returned to him a perfectly well woman and remained in his house two weeks. When this physician and those who knew the woman saw what Christian Science had done for her, a great interest was aroused among them.

They had no understanding of the Science, but many chronic invalids and others who needed help were desirous for the treatment and wished me to go to that place and take their cases. When they wrote to that effect, I sent them word that I could not go, that I had all that I could do at the College. But they would not take "No" for an answer and continued to urge me to go, until finally I asked Mrs. Eddy what had better be done. She replied, "Write them you will go for one week," which I did. I also said I would give them a talk on the Science the first and second evenings after my arrival if they would engage a hall for that purpose and be willing to do something for themselves in subscribing for *The Christian Science Journal* for one year. My object in doing this was first for the aid the *Journal* would be to them after I left them as they were starting in a new and untried way. Then, the *Journal* itself was in its first year of growth and needed our best efforts to support it and extend its circulation. Its worth was gradually seen, but the way must be made for it.

I found these people very ready to do what was asked of them, and the hall was well filled the two evenings I spoke to them. When I was through, people crowded about making appointments for the next day until every minute of the day was spoken for. When the time came, they were there promptly, beginning early in the morning and continuing through the day until late at night, with a room filled with people waiting perhaps two or three hours before they could be seen.

I was staying at the home [where] one who had been my patient [roomed—the patient who] was healed and whose case it was that led the physician above mentioned to think favorably of this method of treatment. She made herself very useful in receiving those who came, and her time was fully taken in this way. I had much sympathy for the large number who came from the surrounding towns begging that I take their cases, whom I had not the time to even see. I then sent a telegram to Boston for help, but could find no one to come. I took little time to eat or sleep. My one desire was to do the best and all I could for those dear people during my short stay with them, and God wonderfully blessed my efforts.

Christian Science was the one topic of conversation in town and on the outbound trains, and much antagonism was expressed by certain clergymen and M.D.'s when their people and patients rejoiced in the proof of the great healing power of Truth and trusted in it for their help. On one occasion a gentleman whose wife and daughter were being benefited by the treatment was met by his minister who bitterly denounced Christian Science and among other things said it was the work of the devil. The gentleman replied, "If it is the work of the devil, then I only wish there were more devils and less ministers." The minister, much amused by his quick wit, took it good-naturedly.

Many who became interested in Christian Science at that time later were teachers and healers themselves, going out into different cities and filling responsible positions, and one was made one of the first Directors of The Mother Church by our Leader.

I remained in New Hampshire eleven days, then returned home to the College. The young lady had gone back to her home in Vermont where her many friends who had known her condition and that she was healed in Christian Science went to see for themselves, for as some of them said, it seemed a miracle had been performed. They were amazed at her appearance of perfect health and strength. The result was an urgent call to go there, and I went for a short time.

I wrote them I would give an informal parlor talk in the evening. Arriving at the time appointed, I was met by the young woman who said there were so many who wanted to hear about Christian Science that I was to speak in a church. She little knew what that meant to me. I felt wholly unprepared to address such a body of people from the platform, having given no special thought as to what I should say as I expected to meet only a comparatively small number in a private house. When we reached the church and I saw a well-filled house, my courage almost failed me. Then I thought, "This is God's work and He will take care of it," and took my place fearlessly, addressing the audience with no difficulty, and many believed.

One, an extreme case of double curvature of the spine, heart disease, and other troubles, whom the doctors had given but a short time to live, was instantaneously healed and soon had class instruction and has since been a successful worker in Christian Science. Another, a case of accident from which the man had long been a sufferer, declared he had come expecting to oppose all that was said, but he not only believed, but was healed. Others expressed their thanks for what the truth had done for them.

August 8, 1884, I again had the great privilege of being taught by Mrs. Eddy, this time in her first Normal class, and September 2, 1884, I opened the first class in Christian Science taught by a Normal class student. This I was at first reluctant to do, having before me only the wonderful, spiritual teachings of our great Leader. I felt how far short I must come, and hesitated to take the step. As she said, she had hard work to get me to teach, until I went to my Bible for my final answer, which was given in such plain terms I could no longer doubt, and immediately I began my work in that line and have continued it to the present day.

One day when I was taking dinner with Mrs. Eddy the doorbell rang and on learning that a lady had called to see her, she said she would not keep her waiting, so left the table and went to her. This lady proved to be a physician who had been to see her some time before and had now come to tell her that she had a chronic trouble of long standing that drugs failed to heal, but that she had been entirely free from it from the day she first met Mrs. Eddy.

December 5, 1887, I entered [another of Mrs. Eddy's classes]. It was a large and interesting class that nearly filled the room, and as we sat waiting for our teacher there were some who felt they could hardly bear the touch of mortal thought about them, so rapt were they in the expectation of what was in store for them through their teacher. As she came into the room her face shone with a light that was heavenly and betokened the spiritual illumination that would come to these waiting students as she taught them the truth of being. She began, as it would seem, by sounding the thought of each one, as one would touch the keys of a piano to get the true tone. She spoke a few words to each in turn until she had gone through the whole class. When she reached me, then I understood, she so perfectly expressed my attitude of thought. What she gave us in that class was wonderful, as were all her teachings. And to be with her and personally taught by her was a greater privilege than words can express. But I have heard her say repeatedly: "They who know (understand) my book, know me."

In the year 1889, when our teacher had decided to close the Massachusetts Metaphysical College at the height of its prosperity, there were those among her students who did not see the wisdom of this move, and three of the number consulted as to what should be done. They said as far as spiritual things were concerned there was no question as to our teacher's judgment and ability, but in matters of business it was not expected she would understand; to close the College when a large number were only waiting the opportunity to enter was to them a great mistake, and they decided it was their duty to go to Concord and advise her what to do.

Accordingly, on the day appointed the three men went to 62 North State Street, Concord, where Mrs. Eddy then resided, and asked to see her. They were told she was busy, but would see them soon. When she entered the room, she sat down and had a few minutes' conversation with them which opened their eyes and their understanding. When she was through, she turned to one and asked what it was he wished to see her about. He hesitated, not knowing what to say, and replied, "Oh, nothing in particular." She then turned to the next one and asked him what it was he wanted, and he said the same—that there was nothing, and so said the third, and as they related this occurrence to me they said they would have been glad if the floor had opened and let them down out of sight. Their own lack was uncovered and they were ashamed of the step they had taken. Surely, "the wisdom of this world is foolishness with God" (I Cor. 3:19).

The following notice of a special meeting of the Massachusetts Metaphysical College Corporation of which I was a member was sent me by the Clerk, Calvin A. Frye, and I was present at this meeting at which the corporation was dissolved:

> 62 N. State Street
> Concord, N.H.
> Oct. 22, 1889

Miss J. S. Bartlett
Dear Sister:
    There will be a business meeting of the Mass. Metaphysical College Corporation, on Tuesday

Oct. 29 at 11 a.m. at 62 N. State St., Concord, N.H.
As business of great importance will be transacted,
you are urgently requested to be present.
Let this be strictly confidential.

C. A. Frye, *Clerk*

Our teacher was much gratified to find the board [of officers of the College] strongly with her in this move.

When our Leader went from Boston to Concord in 1889 she needed to go in order to have an opportunity to revise her book *Science and Health* without the constant interruptions arising from the work at headquarters. It was also time that students should be less dependent upon the watchfulness and care of their teacher and learn to rely more on God. She knew they must learn sooner or later to *guard themselves,* to watch and not be misled, and knowing better than we what her going would mean to us, she dictated the following few lines for me to write, while having a talk with her before leaving: "If there is anything pending for the Church or Association and you feel an inclination of *duty* to go away before it is accomplished, remember that [Malicious Animal Magnetism] suggests these things, then stop and consider the consequences and take it up that your mind not be influenced or swayed from God's line of action and that your Teacher is not with you now to forewarn but God is." I then decided, no matter what the needs might be outside, not to leave my post in Boston.

May 26, 1895, Mrs. Eddy first attended the church service in the new church. She arrived at the church Saturday about twilight and spent the night in the Mother's Room. No one was supposed to know she was in Boston excepting the few it was necessary should know, but Sunday it was soon whispered from one to another as they entered the church that Mrs. Eddy was there, and all were quietly happy, waiting to see her and possibly to hear her. There was no excitement and all were asked to take their seats early in order to clear the vestibule, which they did.

The Original Mother Church, completed in 1894

When about half through the lesson, the Readers stopped and the soft, sweet strains of the organ filled the room as our Leader walked up the aisle to the platform, leaning on the arm of a student. The large audience rose to their feet with one accord and remained standing until she was seated. She was then introduced as the author of *Science and Health* and the Pastor [Emeritus] of The Mother Church, after which a solo was sung by Miss Elsie Lincoln. Our revered Leader then rose to speak while the audience listened with rapt attention, eager to catch every word which fell from the lips of the inspired speaker. We caught the spirit of her words and went out from The Mother Church conscious of the sweet presence of Truth and Love, to commune one with another on the wonderful discourse we had heard and to ponder it in our hearts.

Our Leader remained in the Mother's Room until time to take the five o'clock train to Concord. A special car was engaged for her, the quiet of which she appreciated and enjoyed.

June 5, 1895, I attended the annual meeting of the Massachusetts Metaphysical College Association. One hundred and eighty were present at this meeting, from the different states and Canada. Our Leader and teacher opened the Bible at the sixty-eighth Psalm and sent word to have it read at this meeting. A long, instructive, and beautiful address was also received from her. The address was read twice, after which we returned to our homes feeling we had had a feast of good things and anticipating the greater joy of the morrow in meeting face to face with our beloved Leader.

Early the next day, June 6, we started for Concord. It was a very stormy morning, but the clouds soon began to break away and the day was fine. Our little journey on the special train of six cars was especially harmonious; everyone quietly enjoyed the ride, feeling the Mother-love which was bestowing so much on her children. When we reached Pleasant View, our dear teacher was waiting to receive us, and taking each by the hand, she spoke a few endearing words which we remember because of the love expressed. Her words to me were simply, "Bless you, *dear* Julia."

After she had seen all, she made some general remarks that were most helpful and interesting, then went to her room for a while, but soon returned and we enjoyed a little singing by Miss Lincoln, after which she prepared to go out, leaving us to do as we liked about the house and grounds; and waving her hand and kissing us good-bye, she went with the words, "Parting makes tender." We returned to Boston on the five o'clock special with hearts filled with love and gratitude to the one who with all her worldwide cares and responsibilities still found time to bring us together with her in this loving, helpful, happy way.

It was dear Mrs. Eddy's custom to invite me to visit her from time to time after I was with her in the College, and I have treasured the sweet memories of the hours spent with her when the cares of the day were laid aside as much as possible and we were free to talk of the things we loved to speak of. She was so lovingly thoughtful for my comfort and happiness, and all her conversation was so dear, uplifting, and helpful, it was a joy to be with her.

She was always mindful of the *little* things. No kind act or loving thought escaped her notice and appreciation; such things only helped to brighten her pathway. If it was nothing more than to take her a bouquet of roses, she would think it was so kind of me and would thank me perhaps two or three times, although she had an abundance of flowers on her own grounds. I always felt how little I was doing for her who was doing so much for me and for all mankind.

The last time she invited me to be with her in this way she had many interruptions and I saw how difficult it was for her to get any time from her work. She said she so hoped to be able to visit with me quietly that day. When at the dinner table, we enjoyed her conversation while the students expressed themselves freely. One in speaking of the good life of a certain man whom he knew said, "That is old-fashioned Christianity." She corrected him by saying, "That is *Christianity.*" Again, in speaking of chemicalization, the aggravation of evil in its destruction, I said, "I suppose that is inevitable." Her face lighted up as she smiled and said, "Yes, from your standpoint, but no." Then she expressed herself beyond what I have ever heard her on this subject which brought out so clearly the *allness* of God and the *nothingness* of evil.

I told Mrs. Eddy how much I always enjoyed and appreciated my visits with her, but that I felt I should not take her time and thereby add to her burdens with all she had to attend to, and that if she did not invite me anymore, I would understand, but I would be glad to go at any time I could be of any service to her. I said to her, "I love you, and I know you love me, and I do not have to see you personally to know this." When I saw the beautiful expression that came over her face and heard what she said, I knew what it meant to her and was glad.

I was never invited to visit her again in the old way, and only went when I could be of some help to her or to the Cause.

The last time I saw our dear Leader was a short time before she went from us to personal sense, and the memory of it is very dear and sacred to me. Never was she so tender and loving, and never did I so desire to be to her all that I should and wish that I might do more for her, but I said in talking with her, "You know that I love you, don't you?" She said, "I *well know* that. Yes, I *well know* that."

I little thought that was the last time I should see her personally, but I have never felt that she, our dear Leader, was parted from us, for she had taught us it was not her personality to which we must look for the real, but to the spiritual idea from which there is no separation; and in this way I love to think of her and continue to strive to follow her teachings.

The Star in My Crown of Rejoicing— The Class of 1885

C. LULU BLACKMAN

*P*ersonal contacts with our dearly loved Leader and teacher, Mary Baker Eddy, were limited, as one measures time, but they left pictures and impressions of rare beauty. Memory has not dimmed these but holds them ever clearly defined.

In order to more clearly reveal her graciousness, her compassionate helpfulness, and her marvelous response to my appeal for the light of Truth that finally led me to the relationship of teacher and student, I shall tell of the first coming of Christian Science in my life.

Young in years, yet without hope of healing, I was facing life from the standpoint of inevitable invalidism when, in 1884, a friend living in Chicago brought to my Nebraska home the story of a new method of healing, called "Metaphysical Healing." She could tell nothing about it except that no drugs were used. She was, however, firmly imbued with the assurance that it did heal where all other methods had failed. I was taken to Chicago to receive treatment from one of Mrs. Eddy's students and after two months of treatment was healed.

The day before I returned home I bought a copy of *Science and Health with Key to the Scriptures* by Mary Baker Eddy. There were no Christian Scientists with whom I might discuss this book, nor any to steady my untried footsteps of thought. Mrs. Eddy, through her book, was my only teacher.

At this time, Mrs. Eddy's personality made no appeal to me. It was wholly unknown, and my imagination was not awakened to even a consideration of what manner of woman this might be. I knew only that she was the author of *Science and Health with Key to the Scriptures* and that the time had come when it was imperative that a key of understanding be given me in order that the pages of *Science and Health* might be read with the assurance that there was no perversion of its actual meaning.

It was to me an indisputable fact that no one else could know the real meaning of the book so well as did the writer of the book. She stood to me as "the voice of one crying in the wilderness, Make straight the way of the Lord" (John 1:23). It was to this voice of Truth I made my direct appeal, and it was as the revelator of Truth she answered me.

Up to this point my mental steps were tentative, but they had brought me to the valley of decision. I wrote to ask admission to her class and with the characteristic frankness of youth and inexperience added, "If it is necessary for me to be a dissatisfied and miserable Christian, I am not ready for this instruction, for I am, and always have been, a very happy one."

This letter has always seemed to me my first coming to Mrs. Eddy, and I am sure it was her first knowledge of me. It was purely mental, but I seemed to know, even before her reply reached me, that we had met. As I look back, her answer to this letter seems very characteristic of her mode of thought and method of action. She wrote the letter herself. She offered no rebuke, she attempted no explanation. There was only the simple, loving message, "Come and see."

Later the details were worked out, and I was called to the class that convened September 14, 1885. This is counted, after these many years, the greatest privilege and joy of my life. In Hebrews 11:8 we read that "Abraham, when he was called to go out into a place which he should after receive for an inheritance, obeyed; and he went out, not knowing whither he went." These words fittingly explain my presence in that class, for Mrs. Eddy, with keenest insight, revealed "a city which hath foundations, whose builder and maker is God" (Hebrews 11:10).

When she entered the classroom, I saw her for the first time. Intuitively, the members of the class rose at her entrance, and remained standing until she was seated. She made her way to a slightly raised platform, turned, and faced us. She wore an imported black satin dress heavily beaded with tiny black jet beads, black satin slippers beaded, and had on her rarely beautiful diamonds. These she spoke of in one of the later sessions. She stood before us, slight, graceful of carriage, and exquisitely beautiful. Then, still standing, she faced her class as one who knew herself to be a teacher by divine right. She was every inch the teacher. She turned to the student at the end of the first row and taking direct mental cognizance of this one, plainly knocked at the door of his thought. It was as if a question had been asked and answered, and a benediction given. Then her eyes rested on the next in order and the same recognition was made. This continued until each member of the class was included. No audible word voiced the purely mental contact.

In this class there were those who knew her and loved her—who had been previously taught by her and were trusted helpers upon whom she called. There were those who doubted and questioned, and still others who, even then in the classroom, seemed swayed by antagonism and said within themselves: "This is the heir; come, let us kill him, and the inheritance shall be ours" (Mark 12:7).

There is no question but that the mentality of the class, individual and collective, was uncovered to her. She felt its challenge, and she met it clear-eyed and undismayed. It was as though she dismissed something from her thought, separated herself from the mental contact, and then lifting her eyes in prayer, with one accord, the Lord's Prayer was spoken. The voice of the class said, "Our Father which art in heaven." As one with the class, and yet distinct from it, we heard these words in Mrs. Eddy's voice, "Our *dear* Father which art in heaven."

These were the first words I heard her speak. They were arresting, compelling. There was a lilt of joy in her voice; I had the impression of a child who was unafraid, and a subtle but clear assurance was with me that she dwelt consciously, confidently "in the secret place of the most High" (Psalm 91:1). It was not as though she had gone to the Father in prayer, but rather as though, because she was with the Father, she prayed. In days that followed she gave us the Christian Science teachings on the subject of prayer, but this experience has remained with me as one of my most precious memories. The incident was a "living illustration," and added something that conveyed the very essence of her attitude on prayer.

After this audible repetition of the Lord's Prayer, Mrs. Eddy took her seat and the students resumed theirs. As she began to speak, many of the students opened notebooks and began to write. Instantly she said, "Put up your notebooks." I had written but one sentence and no other was ever added. There were others who refused to consider the command as final and, almost at once, covertly began again to make notes. With eagle eyes she detected the overt act and again repeated the words "Put up your notebooks." All complied; then she resumed her teaching. A little later, one student began again surreptitiously to make notations. Stopping her discourse, Mrs. Eddy for the third time repeated the words emphatically and clearly, and never again was there an effort on the part of any to write down a thought or word that came from this great teacher. She at no time made any explanation of this requirement, but all my days I have blessed her for this ruling, because it compelled us to let the form go so that limited finite statements of Truth might not circumscribe the pinions of her thought. Her impartations transcended the medium of words. Words served only to convey her revelations. She gave both the letter and the spirit, but she took away the letter lest any should substitute it for the wine of the Spirit.

The first three days in the classroom gave overwhelming proof of Mrs. Eddy's understanding of God and her consistent acceptance of the fact that there was none beside Him. In my own experience, she seemed to have obliterated everything I had deemed substantial and actual. The word "God"—"God"—"God" was repeated over and over in my consciousness to the exclusion of all else.

Mrs. Eddy awakened us to the realization that she taught no mere theory but the practical, living Truth when she closed the third lesson with these words: "Now go home and take your first patient." In my own estimation I was not ready to take a patient. She had taken away my Lord, and as yet I knew not the God she had revealed. It was a great relief to remember that I was a complete stranger in Boston and so could not possibly be called upon to give a treatment. Not willful disobedience but stress of circumstances would exempt me from the necessity or opportunity of taking a patient. The relief was short-lived, for when I opened the door of my rooming place a member of the family was found to be very ill with erysipelas. When he saw that I was making haste to escape to my room he called to me: "If you can do anything for me, why don't you do it?"

The swift healing that followed my obedience to Mrs. Eddy's demand that I take my first patient gave me a keen insight into her characteristic faith in the power of the Word of God when applied through the Science she was giving to the world. She had arranged no details, provided no patients. She gave the command and knew God would "supply the wisdom and the occasion for a victory over evil" (*Science and Health,* p. 571).

The experience connected with this case of healing revealed to me something of the immensity of the work Mrs. Eddy had accomplished in her three days in the classroom. She had not taken up the question of animal magnetism but she had established for us her concept of God, and this true concept of God rescued and defended me from the devil and his adversaries in a time of such temptation as I had never before known. Suggestions taking form in words declared that I did not know enough of the Christian Science method to use it and declared that there was a power in my own mind that I could use instead. Error pleaded with me to substitute mortal mind for immortal Mind, arguing that mortal mind was my natural habitat, and that immortal Mind was too transcendental to avail.

I had been precipitated into a seeming mental realm where the supposititious forces of evil sought to establish the claim to equal or transcend the power of God. I realized that there was a greater question here than that of mere physical healing. The decision to rely upon divine Mind alone was made, and I answered the tempter, "I will not resort to willpower, even if the young man dies." Then as a ministering angel, this scriptural verse came to me: "Put off thy shoes from off thy feet, for the place whereon thou standest is holy ground" (Exodus 3:5). I had forgotten the patient, but as I turned to leave the room I saw he was sleeping peacefully and that complete healing had taken place.

Thus Mrs. Eddy revealed herself to us through the power of the Word. She effaced the sense of her personality so completely that she thought, spoke, and acted from the standpoint of her oneness with the Father. In *Unity of Good* (p. 48), referring to God, Mrs. Eddy says: "He sustains my individuality. Nay, more—He *is* my individuality and my Life." So many statements made in her writings are illuminated by the fact that she lived the truth she spoke—lived it so simply, humbly, and completely that she proved what the Master meant when he said, "I and my Father are one" (John 10:30).

In subsequent lessons, she took up the question of evil. I shall never forget Mrs. Eddy as she appeared when she turned from the contemplation of all good to the supposititious claim of evil, called devil. It was a revelation of Truth, but it was also an unconscious revelation of the price of learning Love which this woman had paid through vital experience, through the things she had suffered—because of the exaltation of God in her own consciousness. The picture of this loved teacher as she shared the hemlock cup with her half-comprehending students is word painted in this paragraph on page 48 of *Science and Health:* "Remembering the sweat of agony which fell in holy benediction on the grass of Gethsemane, shall the humblest or mightiest disciple murmur when he drinks from the same cup, and think, or even wish, to escape the exalting ordeal of sin's revenge on its destroyer? Truth and Love bestow few palms until the consummation of a life-work."

Perhaps the presence of one who was soon to stand before the world as an opponent of Mrs. Eddy and a refuter of her teachings, in the effort to usurp her place as Leader, intensified the lights and shadows to this class. Silently and audibly this one sought to carry the students with her; when nearing the close of the class she became openly defiant. I saw and heard Mrs. Eddy deal with this state of consciousness. Her loving-kindness, gentle patience, and consecration of purpose, revealed her character. In *Miscellaneous Writings* (p. 254), Mrs. Eddy questions: "Should not the loving warning, the far-seeing wisdom, the gentle entreaty, the stern rebuke have been heeded, in return for all that love which brooded tireless over their tender years? for all that love that hath fed them with Truth,—even the bread that cometh down from heaven,—as the mother-bird tendeth her young in the rock-ribbed nest of the raven's callow brood!"

I count it a privilege to bear witness that "the loving warning, the far-seeing wisdom, the gentle entreaty, the stern rebuke" were not lacking. She reversed the sense of evil and made plain the meaning of David's words: "Whither shall I go from thy spirit? or whither shall I flee from thy presence? If I ascend up into heaven, thou art there: if I make my bed in hell, behold, thou art there" (Psalm 139:7, 8).

Mrs. Eddy always conveyed the impression to me that what she knew of evil had not come to her through the study of evil but through her exaltation of God.

The word "transparency" seems best to express my remembrance of Mrs. Eddy's personal appearance. I have never seen anyone with such swiftly changing expression, one who seemed so at one with the thought she presented. Sometimes she gave me the impression of having lived forever—that no years could measure her age; and again all sense of time seemed wiped out and she looked like a vision of youth. The beauty of her thought expressed in the physical illustrates her statement in *Science and Health* (p. 248), "Immortal Mind feeds the body with supernal freshness and fairness, supplying it with beautiful images of thought and destroying the woes of sense which each day brings to a nearer tomb."

She characterized divine loveliness in these moments of supernal freshness, and gave proof of her statement, "Beauty is a thing of life, which dwells forever in the eternal Mind and reflects the charms of His goodness in expression, form, outline, and color" (*Science and Health,* p. 247). I count it a blessed experience to have seen this radiancy of Soul, this glory of immortality untouched by time.

Mrs. Eddy realized that those coming to Boston from a great distance felt a sense of disappointment that no church services were being held because of a vacation period. This might mean that some would never have the opportunity to hear her preach. Her gracious thoughtfulness on our behalf was evinced by her inviting us to meet on Sunday morning, when she would give to us her exposition of the ninety-first Psalm.

My appreciation of this has ever been an increasing one, and an added proof of her boundless giving.

When we came close to the time of our parting, she exemplified mother-love to a marvelous degree. She told us plainly of the serpent sense that ever pursues the spiritual idea. There was admonition and warning and a great desire manifested *to protect* the Christ-idea from the destroying Herod thought. She quoted these words from Matthew 10:16: "Behold, I send you forth as sheep in the midst of wolves: be ye therefore wise as serpents, and harmless as doves." I remember her statement, "There are no short cuts in Christian Science," and she said, as I recall, "I have taken you up into the mount; I have showed you the promised land"—and then she added with finality, but also with infinite tenderness—*"but you will have to walk every step of the way to get there."*

At no time had Mrs. Eddy remained in the room or given op-

60

portunity for speaking to her after she finished her lesson for the day. She invariably left the room before the students rose from their seats. The only exception to this procedure came at the close of the final lesson. Then she stepped to the edge of the slightly raised platform and waited for each member of the class to come and say good-bye. She shook hands with each one and spoke directly to each. I have no way of knowing what she said to others, but I know the message she gave me. As she held my hand she looked directly into my eyes and said, "Thou art mine, saith the Lord, and none shall pluck you from out my hand."

Only once after leaving Boston did I again see Mrs. Eddy. This was a few years later when a classmate and I went to Concord, New Hampshire. Because at that time friends and strangers alike were too insistent in their attempted invasion of her privacy, we decided to make no attempt to see her, or even to pass by her Pleasant View home.

However, when leaving Concord we walked to the railway station, and all unexpectedly we saw her carriage coming toward us. She smiled and bowed. Before we had gone many blocks the carriage again intercepted our way. This time Mrs. Eddy leaned forward, smiled, and waved her hand. It was a charming incident, a gracious greeting, and my last vision of the teacher whom I love dearly.

In my remembrance of Mrs. Eddy there is no one thing that impressed me more than the faith she had in her own words—her faith in the truth of the Science she has given to mankind. In *Miscellaneous Writings* (p. 99) Mrs. Eddy writes, "In no other one thing seemed Jesus of Nazareth more divine than in his faith in the immortality of his words." Mrs. Eddy's faith in the correctness of her interpretation of divine Science, when all the world doubted, transcended human belief, and revealed a "conscious, constant capacity to understand God" (*Science and Health,* p. 209). This faith on her part left a deep impression on me. It seemed to stand back of every word she spoke and to glorify her manifest sincerity.

Today countless numbers give loving recognition of the part the Discoverer and Founder of Christian Science has had in bringing them to conscious at-one-ment with God. Her identification with Truth is so fixed in my thought that no sense of absence, separation, or time touches my remembrance. She stands as a reflection of ever-present Truth. I love her more today than I did yesterday, simply because through demonstration I understand her better. She is my teacher, and to have had the privilege of being taught by her is the star in my crown of rejoicing.

Loved Memories of Mary Baker Eddy

ABIGAIL DYER THOMPSON

"The lives of great men and women are miracles of patience and perseverance. Every luminary in the constellation of human greatness, like the stars, comes out in the darkness to shine with the reflected light of God," writes Mary Baker Eddy in her message on "Fidelity" in *Miscellaneous Writings* (p. 340). Her own life has radiated the greatest spiritual illumination in modern times, and more and more with the passing years do we appreciate the value of her example.

August of 1886 marks an outstanding experience in my childhood memory. My mother had been called to her first class of instruction under Mrs. Eddy, and I accompanied her to Boston. Because we stopped near the College in a private home, I saw our Leader almost daily. I shall never forget the great joy that I experienced when I first met her. On one of my earliest visits to Boston my mother and I attended a Christian Science service in Chickering Hall. To our great happiness the sermon that morning was preached by our beloved Leader, and at its close I had the pleasure of going with my mother to the platform and speaking with Mrs. Eddy. I can close my eyes and see her even now as she stood before that congregation, graceful, earnest, impassioned, with a ring of sincerity in her voice that held her listeners spellbound as long as she continued talking.

No one who has ever seen our Leader could forget her personal charm. In the days when I first knew her there was the vigor and buoyancy of youth in her manner. Her hair was dark brown and her complexion as shell pink and clear as that of a child. Her dark, luminous eyes deepened and shone with such a rapid

Chickering Hall, Boston, Massachusetts

change of expression that it was difficult to determine their exact color. During a trip to Europe, I wrote to our Leader asking for a photograph that she considered a good likeness, as I wished to have a porcelain portrait painted in Dresden. Three pictures came by return mail. Upon reaching this country, and before returning to my home, I called upon Mrs. Eddy at Pleasant View and showed her the miniature. After studying it for a few moments she remarked, in substance, The eyes are very brown. Then she added, Artists usually want to paint my eyes brown, but no one seems to know their exact color. Walking to the tower window, she said, Come into the light, dear, and see what you think of them. After looking intently for a moment, I exclaimed, Why, they are a deep gray-blue, and I always supposed they were brown. However, I really think that, like the constant change of expression in her face, her eyes at times took on different hues.

It was my blessed privilege to be a member of our Leader's last class. Through the influence of my mother's deep appreciation of Mrs. Eddy as God-inspired in her leadership, I was prepared to follow with absorbing interest every word of her teaching. I can never be grateful enough for having had awakened in me during my childhood years a love and reverence for the Discoverer and Founder of Christian Science that opened my mind to hear and gave me an overwhelming desire to lay hold on the things of Spirit.

As I look back to many inspiring interviews with our beloved Leader, I cherish them as the most exalted moments of my life. She spoke of spiritual things with an intimacy that revealed her vision vividly to one's consciousness, leaving a deep and lasting impression that was not unlike what the disciples must have felt on the mount of transfiguration.

At one time when our Leader was talking with me of the importance of more and better healing work in our movement, she asked if I had been careful to keep a record of my own cases of healing for future reference. I said it had never occurred to me to take any particular note of them. To this Mrs. Eddy replied with earnestness, as near as I can recall her words, You should, dear, be faithful to keep an exact record of your demonstrations, for you never know when they might prove of value to the Cause in meeting attacks on Christian Science. Then she added, sadly, I regret to say that in the rush of a crowded life it is easy to forget even important experiences, and I am sorry that this has been true of much of my best healing work.

Dear, blessed helper of the whole world, little did she realize that at that very moment she was talking to one who owed years of abounding health to the skill of her own healing demonstrations!

On another occasion when I was calling at Pleasant View, I repeated to our Leader a statement that had been made to me by a Christian Science worker who, at the time, was standing in a position of prominence. I could not reconcile the thought to my own understanding of metaphysics, and had determined the next time I saw Mrs. Eddy to ask her if I was right in refusing to accept it. She said, in substance, Your own interpretation is entirely correct, and in this connection I want to impress upon you one fact: no matter how exalted a position a Christian Scientist may occupy in the movement, never accept what he may say as valid unless you can verify the statement in our textbook, *Science and Health with Key to the Scriptures*.

When I first knew Mrs. Eddy I was a happy, friendly child, with just enough shyness to make me a good listener when with older people, and above everything else I loved Christian Science. Intuitively our Leader must have felt this fact, because otherwise, in the stress of her busy life, undoubtedly I should not have received so many evidences of her loving interest.

Her kindnesses were shown in such small ways as this. The first two or three times I came to Boston with my mother, she had her correspondence forwarded to the Massachusetts Metaphysical College and I called there each day for the mail. Frequently Mrs. Eddy would pass through the hall when I was sorting the letters, and invariably she would pause to talk with me for a few moments. At the time of mother's first class, my sister and I were invited to spend a delightful evening with her.

In my frequent visits to Boston I enjoyed many interviews with this great woman, and one time my mother and I were privileged to be her guests overnight at Pleasant View.

I stand before you tonight a living witness who can bear glad testimony to the healing efficacy of this marvelous woman's realization of Truth. Twice during my childhood I was instantaneously healed through the tender ministrations of our precious Leader from what the physicians would have regarded as hopeless physical conditions. From babyhood I had been an extremely delicate child, with three generations of serious lung trouble as a background on my father's side. On one occasion, previous to going East with my mother, I developed a severe cold which left me with a deep, hollow-sounding cough. As soon as Mrs. Eddy heard the cough she quickly detected the seriousness of the condition and gave me one treatment, which was all I needed to eradicate completely every vestige of the lung difficulty. The rasping cough ceased at once, and not only did this distressing condition yield, but the whole mortal law which lay back of the trouble was broken, and through the years that followed I have rejoiced in complete freedom from any return of this so-called family inheritance.

A year or so later, when we were again in Boston, I experienced another instantaneous healing as the result of our Leader's powerful realization of Truth. This time I was stricken suddenly and confined to my bed with a most distressing hip trouble. For more than a week, night and day, I lay racked with pain, steadily growing weaker, until the symptoms appeared most alarming. My mother then turned to our Leader for counsel. Mrs. Eddy, knowing that she had been carrying the case alone and at the same time giving me constant nursing care, probably felt that the condition was becoming too real to her thought, and to relieve this situation advised putting another practitioner on the case. The one she suggested worked earnestly for a few days, but the suffering continued unabated.

Finally the pain became so intense that my dear, courageous mother found herself overwhelmed with discouragement and fear as to the outcome, and in this extremity, after a night of almost unbearable suffering, she hastened at five o'clock in the morning to Mrs. Eddy's home. Mr. Frye talked with her in the hall, explaining that it would be impossible to see our Leader until a couple of hours later. However, Mrs. Eddy heard them talking and, recognizing my mother's voice, stepped to the head of the stairs and listened to the conversation. When mother entered my room a few moments later, even before reaching the bedside, she was greeted with the cheery ring of my voice calling to her the welcome message, "Mother, I am better!" And soon we both realized with the greatest joy that I was not only better but completely healed.

Returning to our Leader's home at the appointed hour, my mother bore the joyful news of the sudden change in my condition, to which Mrs. Eddy smilingly replied, in substance: I overheard your conversation this morning and said to myself, It is time for me to step in on this case and save that child. Hurrying to my room, I dropped into a chair and immediately reached out to God for the healing.

So rapid was my recovery that in a few days I was able to make the journey of fifteen hundred miles to our home in the Middle West in perfect comfort. Through the many years that have followed I have rejoiced in abounding health, and from the depths of a grateful heart I give the entire credit for my freedom to the completeness and permanency of our Leader's realization of the healing power of God.

As I think back through the years that I knew Mrs. Eddy, I always feel that the secret of her great achievements could be explained on no other basis than her at-one-ment with God and her boundless spirit of universal love for all mankind. Prior to my taking class instruction with Mrs. Eddy, this was beautifully expressed to me once by our Leader in conversation, in the words she used to describe her healing work, which, as near as I can recall, were as follows: I saw the love of God encircling the universe and man, filling all space, and that divine Love so permeated my own consciousness that I loved with Christlike compassion everything I saw. This realization of divine Love called into expression "the beauty of holiness, the perfection of being" (*Science and Health*, p. 253), which healed, and regenerated, and saved all who turned to me for help.

The way Mrs. Eddy said the word "Love" made me feel that she must have loved even a blade of grass under her feet. The spiritual healing that Mary Baker Eddy started more than three quarters of a century ago is increasing in its abundance year by year. As the harvest song of gratitude for Christian Science rises throughout the world, her name will be enshrined in the hearts of humanity; therefore it is natural that her followers are eager, in the words of the Scriptures, to "give her of the fruit of her hands; and let her own works praise her in the gates" (Proverbs 31:31).

Reminiscences of Mary Baker Eddy

ANNIE M. KNOTT

*I*n January 1882, I came to Chicago, after four years spent in England, the greater part of that time having been in London. Soon thereafter someone I knew had treatment in Christian Science from one of the first students of Mary Baker Eddy in Chicago, and my friend was healed in a few days of a long-standing ailment. Nor was this all, for I was told that the claim was made that Christian Science was the method practiced by Christ Jesus and taught to his disciples. My comment was that if this were true there was nothing in the world worth troubling about. I soon found that it was true! Many cases of healing came to my notice, and as I began to study *Science and Health with Key to the Scriptures* by Mrs. Eddy, every sentence brought conviction as in the study of geometry, and proofs multiplied.

My first meeting with Mrs. Eddy was in February 1887, when I had the privilege of studying in her Normal class. It was a very cold morning, and when I entered the College at 571 Columbus Avenue there were a number of other students removing their wraps and going upstairs to the classroom. As I did not expect to meet anyone whom I knew, I paid little attention to those who were coming in, but presently a very sweet voice greeted me by asking my name. In a moment I realized that I was in Mrs. Eddy's presence, and could scarcely find my voice as I thought upon the moral and spiritual greatness of the woman who was speaking to me. I gave my name, and then realized that she held my hand in her own with gentle pressure, and asked if I was not cold. I think I responded in the negative, although to the senses I was uncomfortably cold, but my thought was immediately lifted above the physical to the realization of that which I had been cherishing for a good while.

As I looked into Mrs. Eddy's face I saw at once the wonderful character expressed so far as the human face and form can express it. The graceful figure, the beautiful hands, the well-shaped head with its dignified poise, the masses of beautiful brown hair, which at that time showed no trace of gray, and above all the wonderful eyes, with the depths of thought and feeling which looked out beyond the human sense of things into spiritual realities. With all this flooding my consciousness I realized that Mrs. Eddy was no stranger to me, because for more than two years I had been learning to know her through her great message to humanity, *Science and Health with Key to the Scriptures.* From the first hour almost that I had opened the book I was aware that it was for me a complete key to the Scriptures, and not only so, but I had proved through its teachings that Christian Science is indeed the promised Comforter, and that the healing work practiced by Jesus and taught to his disciples had become a present reality.

When I entered the classroom, students from different parts of the country were introducing themselves to each other, and in a few moments Mrs. Eddy herself entered and took her place at one end of the classroom. Here I ought to say that I had scarcely left her presence to ascend the stairs when I was aware of a warm glow in my hands, and all sense of chilliness and discomfort had gone. Not only was this true, but in the classroom I could not help observing that my hands seemed to be changed, and the redness and roughness due to the cold outside had entirely vanished, nor did it ever return. This, however, was a small thing compared with the searching questions which opened up the thought of the students to the actual work of the class. On many occasions I have noticed Mrs. Eddy's remarkable keenness in observing the thought of those in her presence, and on this morning it gave me a never-to-be-forgotten lesson.

Mrs. Eddy had only spoken for a few moments when she evidently discerned mentally some thought not in line with Christian Science, and so she asked whether anyone in the class believed in what was known as spiritualism, or, to put it otherwise, believed that communications from those who had passed on were possible. In asking this she said that if any of those who were present did so believe, they might raise their hands. One lady who sat near me did so, and instead of a stern rebuke or criticism Mrs. Eddy smiled gently and said: "Thank you. Your honesty in responding to my question will be of much service to you in gaining a clearer sense of Truth in these lessons." Mrs. Eddy then asked her what was the basis for her belief in spiritualism. The lady at once responded that she had had evidence of it on several occasions, that she had had communications from her own mother, who had passed on some years before. Mrs. Eddy looked serious for a few moments, and then asked the student if she had not at times experienced sickness and suffering, perhaps even after becoming acquainted with the teachings of Christian Science. The lady admitted that she had had such experiences, and Mrs. Eddy went on to ask her if they did not seem very real indeed. To this the student responded in the affirmative, when Mrs. Eddy said in substance: The evidences of which you have spoken are on the same line with the sense evidence of disease and pain. Neither the one nor the other deals with spiritual reality, but only with varying phases of mortal belief.

The student then began to contend that the Bible gave a number of instances of communications from those who had passed on, and cited first the story of the witch of Endor. This was quickly disposed of, for Mrs. Eddy showed that it only represented a prevailing belief in spiritualism, that even Saul's edict that witches were to be put to death indicated a widespread belief in the necromancy of that day, and that when Saul, in his human extremity, turned away from God, he fell into the deep pit of superstition and disobedience to divine law, and lost the way of Truth. This was made so lucid by a few words from Mrs. Eddy that no argument was needed, but the student then offered the experience of Saul of Tarsus on his way to Damascus to persecute Jesus' followers. The student claimed that Jesus personally called to this man, better known to us as Paul, and so illumined his consciousness with truth that he was turned from his erring ways and began to be a follower of the Nazarene Teacher. Mrs. Eddy expressed some surprise at this argument, and asked if any others in the class believed that this had been a personal appearance. Without waiting for an answer she called upon a member of the class who was seated in front of her chair, and asked how he regarded it. He spoke at some length and explained that before coming into Christian Science he had believed that it was the personal Jesus who addressed Paul, but that after studying *Science and Health with Key to the Scriptures,* he had come to see that it was a subjective experience, that the eternal Christ spoke to Paul and wakened him from his erroneous thinking, and that while Paul probably continued for some time to think that it was the personal Jesus who had addressed him, nevertheless Christ Jesus became to him the Way-shower to Truth and Love. Mrs. Eddy commended the answer, and with a few kindly words to the student who had been the means of opening up this discussion, she went on with the regular teaching.

The following is a statement which Mrs. Eddy made in class, and which was copied by Mr. Frye and given to the members of the class: "In treating against malpractice the student must not call the names of individuals because he cannot know who is sinning always but he can make sin to himself nothing through divine Science. Declare positively, mortal minds cannot harm me or my patients. One Mind governs all harmoniously." We were to declare daily, "I cannot suffer from others' sins for sin is its own punisher and I will not sin, then I am free from suffering."

The closing lesson followed on something of the same lines as the others, and for myself I could hardly say that it left me with a happy sense of the experiences which might come at any time. Within a few days, however, I was back at my work in Detroit, and was called upon to heal some more difficult cases than any I had before encountered in my two years' practice. I was even astonished at the results in these cases, and at this late day love to think upon the spiritual strength which had come to me from this teaching of our Leader.

The second day after my return I was called to treat a man who was said to be violently insane, so much so that three men had to be in the room with him all the time. The lady who came to ask me to take the case was not a Christian Scientist, nor were any of the family, but the case was so desperate that someone had suggested Christian Science treatment to them. I said to the lady who came for me that I could not possibly go to the case as I had some very important healing work at the time. The lady was greatly disturbed and said, "You call yourself a Christian woman and yet you refuse to come where the need is so great." I replied, "No, I cannot refuse if you put it on that basis. I will come as soon as possible."

When I reached the home three men were waiting in the hall downstairs to go up and relieve the others who were in the man's room, and I was told that it would not be possible for me to enter the room at all, that he would become so violent if he saw a stranger that he could not be held at all. I, however, was given a quiet room near him and remained for over a half hour. Mrs. Eddy's wonderful teaching in the recent class became so clear to me that I felt I could raise the dead if called upon to do so. After I left the room I was told that the man became calm and peaceful after my treatment began, although neither the man himself nor those in the room knew of my being in the house. He spoke to his son in a perfectly rational way and said he must have been very sick, and told the son to call his mother. The wife came up full of thankfulness and sat down beside him. The others were all asked to leave the room as there was no need of their services any longer. Although he had not been asleep for a week and drugs had failed to have any influence, he fell asleep and remained quiet for over twenty-four hours. When he waked up the next day he was disturbed for a short time, but I was hastily summoned to the house and again treated him with good results as on the first occasion. There was no return of this dread illness, and I never saw the man until a few years passed, when I saw him Sunday after Sunday in our Christian Science church.

Within a few weeks after the Normal class of February 1887, I received a letter from Mrs. Eddy inviting me to be present at a meeting of students to be held April 13, of that year. When this request came I felt that I could not well spare the time or money to return to Boston so soon after I had been there, and wrote her to that effect. (I afterwards learned that the majority of those who had been asked to come on for this gathering had sent our Leader word that they would be unable to comply with her request, and some did not even take the trouble to notify her of their unreadiness to respond to her request.) Within a short time, when I was about to give treatment to a patient who had called, there was delivered to me by the American Express Company the following letter from Mrs. Eddy:

> 571 Columbus Ave.
> Boston, March 31, 1887
>
> My dear Student
> I have gotten up this N. C. S. A. [National Christian Scientist Association] for you and the life of the Cause. I have something important to say to you, a message from God. Will you not meet this one request of your teacher and let *nothing* hinder it? If you do not I shall never make another to you and give up the struggle.
> Lovingly Your Teacher
> M B Eddy

It is needless to say that this message from our Leader dispelled the thought which was seeking to hinder students from responding to their teacher's request, and within a few minutes I was hastening to the Western Union office to wire Mrs. Eddy that I would without fail come to Boston as she had requested. This seemed to call for a sacrifice of time and money, but the experience has always been remembered as a vital step in my progress. Mrs. Eddy's address at the meeting of her students in Tremont Temple was wonderful, and the only regret I can ever feel in connection with the gathering is that it was not published, but only a few hints of it given in the *Journal*.* I also learned on this occasion the lesson which we need to think upon many times, that simple obedience to any righteous requirement in our Cause brings unstinted reward. Throughout the year I did everything in my power to be ready for the gathering in Chicago in June 1888. It was at this time, however, that I heard Mrs. Eddy declare that unless students of Christian Science waked up to the need of the hour, "this Truth would again be lost and buried beneath the rubbish of the centuries."

On the morning of April 14, 1887, I had the privilege of an interview with Mrs. Eddy at the College. This was more than I expected, and her words to me on that occasion made a deep impression upon my thought. Mrs. Eddy began the interview by asking me if I was clear on the great truth that God does not know evil, which she had sought to impress upon us in the Normal class of the previous February. I replied that I thought I did remember her teaching very distinctly, and then she went on to say: "If you stood in front of a mirror, and there was a hole in your dress or a pin in your dress, it would be in the reflection, would it not?" I answered, "Yes." She then said, "It would not be possible to get it out of the reflection so long as it was in the original, would it?" I answered, "No." She said, "You are clear about this, are you?" I replied, "I think I am." She then went on: "Now God never changes, does He? He is eternally the same." To this I again responded, "Yes." She again went on, "Now if God were conscious of sickness, sin, and death, we could never expect to overcome them, for the divine consciousness does not change, and we could never remove from the reflection that which

---

The Christian Science Journal, Vol. 5 (May 1887), pp. 98–100.

is in the original." She again asked me to answer her, which I did, seeing as I had never seen before the vital importance of gaining a clear sense of this truth. This was the substance of the interview, but I have thought of it many times in the years since then, as mortal mind puts up a tremendous argument that God must know evil in order to help us in overcoming it, whereas the opposite is the case.

This same day our Leader asked her students to meet with her at the College, and after talking to them for some time she gave them the privilege of asking her questions, to which no one responded. I myself for a long time regretted my silence on this occasion. Mrs. Eddy mentions this incident on page 137 of *Miscellaneous Writings*.

I had the privilege of again seeing our dear Leader and listening to her words at the meeting in Chicago, June 1888, of the National Christian Scientist Association. Two sessions were held in the First Methodist Church in Chicago, and these were attended only by Mrs. Eddy's own students or by others who had received class instruction from them, the teachers vouching for their own pupils. Mrs. Eddy herself was on the platform, and patiently answered the many questions which were asked from the floor in regard to the healing work, also to the relations of teachers and their students. Her answers always directed thought to the demands of Principle and the need for the maintenance and advance of our great Cause. Besides the sessions held by Mrs. Eddy for her students only, I listened to her wonderful address at the National Convention in Central Music Hall on June 14, which is to be found in *Miscellaneous Writings* under the title "Science and the Senses." To me it was wonderful beyond words, and with the passing of the years it seems no less so. I was, of course, present at the reception at the Palmer House on the evening of that day, and I may say that the reports of the meeting in Central Music Hall and also of the reception at the Palmer House were freely if not very correctly given by the Chicago papers, quoted in *The Christian Science Journal*. Nothing could, however, hinder the great spiritual awakening which came to all who attended these meetings from extending over the whole world, with the firm conviction that the Christ-healing had come again through Christian Science.

Mrs. Eddy speaks of these meetings in the article "Loyal Christian Scientists," which begins on page 275 of *Miscellaneous Writings*. Toward the close of this article she says that she had been "gradually withdrawing from active membership in the Christian Scientist Association." To me it is beyond question that the work of the National Association had all been intended to prepare thought for the development of the Christian Science Church, which later was called The Mother Church, which, of course, includes all of its branches.

Mrs. Eddy early discovered that humanity needed not only to know God but needed a church. Moses knew this and accomplished wonders in the way of its establishment. To the Jewish people the Ten Commandments were undoubtedly the basis of all law and order, and we may rejoice that in the church which Mrs. Eddy established she emphasized the importance of the Decalogue in every way. In my own work most of the healing was brought about quickly, but those healed remained in their old churches because at that time we had not a church of our own in Detroit to which we could invite them; consequently those who were healed made little or no progress. Some, however, became students, and in attending the students' meetings they were made ready for withdrawing from their former churches, and for becoming members of the Church of Christ, Scientist. This, however, called for very earnest work not only in Boston but throughout the entire Field, yet it was more and more clearly seen that Christian Science churches alone could establish and maintain the Christ-healing.

In October 1888, Mrs. Eddy invited me to call on her at her home, 385 Commonwealth Avenue, and she spent over an hour with me, saying that I must begin to hold public services in Detroit and to preach sermons.

After this lengthy interview when I rose to leave, Mrs. Eddy took my hand and said, "Now, will you do what I have told you?" To which I replied that I would "try." To this Mrs. Eddy responded very firmly, "No, that is not enough. Will you *do* it?" And of course the only proper response was to say "Yes!" And Mrs. Eddy's closing words were, "Then, do not forget!" For a time after my return to Detroit I preached sermons in accordance with Mrs. Eddy's instructions. Many, however, of those who had become interested and were studying our textbook, *Science and Health with Key to the Scriptures,* did not wish to leave their former churches, in some cases because of their families, but in reality they did not readily see what it meant to separate themselves from religious bodies who believed that man is material and governed by material law. Those, however, who were gaining the truth more quickly did not hesitate, but were willing to leave their families and attend Christian Science services.

On October 5, 1892, I attended a meeting in Boston called for the purpose of carrying forward the organization of The Mother Church under its present form of government. The meeting was held in Steinert Hall, 62 Boylston Street, when fifty-seven persons signed the roll of membership, myself among them. At the close of the meeting I was quietly invited to visit Mrs. Eddy the next day at her home at Pleasant View, Concord, and I may add that my sister, Mrs. Isabella M. Stewart, C. S. D., of Toronto, was asked to accompany me on this trip.

We were made happy beyond words by this great privilege, and when we reached our Leader's home we met there six other Normal students who had come to share this blessing. As our dear teacher entered the room we could not help being impressed by her grace and dignity, and the evidence of spiritual growth which is often more apparent than the physical growth of a child from year to year. While to the outward sense her hair had become white, evidence to us of the tremendous efforts called for in ascending the mount of revelation, the tone of the spiritual authority based on her wonderful understanding of Truth was the most impressive thing I for one had ever felt. She greeted us lovingly, then asked Mrs. Sargent to bring her *Science and Health,* which she did at once.

The students who were present listened earnestly while our beloved Leader read to us these impressive words from *Science and Health* (page 101 of the 70th edition, lines 19–24): "When we realize that there is but one Mind, the divine law of loving our neighbors as ourselves is unfolded to us; whereas a belief in many ruling minds hinders man's normal drift towards the one Mind, one God, and leads human thought into opposite channels, where selfishness reigns" (page 205 of the present edition). As she read this to us from our inspired textbook, it seemed as if those few lines alone furnished the rule for working out every human problem, no matter how difficult it might seem, and especially the marvelous words, "man's normal drift towards the one Mind, one God." Her wonderful understanding rang out in every word as she read this passage. She pointed out to us without hesitation, as Christ Jesus had done in his day, the attacks of error to which her followers would be subjected, but at the same time she reminded us constantly of the utter powerlessness of error to hinder the progress of Christian Science.

Toward the close of her remarks she said that we must never fear evil, no matter what the seeming might be. And then with a radiant smile, she added that her students thought too much about evil, and often in belief gave it too much power. She went on to say that when error knocks at the door, they sometimes open the door to see what it wants, but Mother did not do that; she knew in advance what it wanted and kept the door shut; but that after her students had opened the door, they had to get the intruder out, and the great thing was to keep error out. At the close of her remarks, before saying good-bye to us she said: "If you, my dear students, could but see the grandeur of your outlook, the infinitude of your hope, and the infinite capabilities of your being, you would do what? You would let error destroy itself." This statement has been passed out a good many times by some of those who were present on that occasion, with slight variations. I wrote it down in this form immediately on going back to the hotel where I was stopping. The interview lasted for nearly two hours, and to several of those who were present it seemed like a whole course of lessons.

At the close our dear Leader invited us to go upstairs with her and see her rooms, especially her study, and then she took us out on the balcony to see the fine view in every direction. One of the students present turned to her suddenly and said, "Mrs. Eddy, won't you point out to us the place where you were born?" To this Mrs. Eddy responded in her characteristic way, and with a radiant smile said, "Oh, I never was born, but if you mean Mary, well, Bow is over there," at the same time indicating with her finger the direction in which we could look to see what would humanly be called her birthplace.

Between 1890 and 1898 it was my duty to represent the Christian Scientists at the Michigan State Capitol in opposition to medical legislation which if enacted would have restricted the practice of Christian Science in the state. On one of these occasions I addressed the legislature, declaring myself "a student of the Rev. Mary Baker Eddy, the Discoverer and Founder of Christian Science." The legislature thereupon acted favorably to protect Christian Scientists in their constitutional right to religious freedom.

Birthplace of Mary Baker Eddy, Bow, New Hampshire

Some time after this when I was visiting Mrs. Eddy, I told her of this experience, and asked her if I did right in using her name and speaking of myself as her student when I addressed the legislature, and she replied that I had done exactly right.

The following is in a letter which I received from her, dated May 10, 1897, in regard to the great victory in the legislature at this time:

She wrote: "Darling, 'Scots, wha hae wi' Wallace bled'—have a moral force innate. Thank God, and my faithful Annie for this brave just defense of Christian Science."

During these years the Christian Science movement was advancing wonderfully, and in 1898 Mrs. Eddy established the Board of Lectureship, my own name being among the appointees.

In January 1899, I was invited to see our Leader at Pleasant View, and had the inestimable privilege of a long interview with her. She asked how I was succeeding in the lecture work, and I told her I had had very few calls up to that time. I added that even personal friends who were members of Christian Science churches wrote me that while they would be glad to hear me, people in general preferred to have a man lecture for them, and so I was temporarily at least like a "briefless barrister." At this point Mrs. Eddy spoke in her usual energetic manner and said it would not do to let that argument stand, that she had appointed me after due consideration, and that it rested with me to make good. Her words were these: "You must rise to the altitude of true womanhood, and then the whole world will want you as it wants Mother." She said further, "I would like to know who has the most intellect, the man or the woman?" And then she laughingly added: "There is not any such thing as intellect, but I mean who reflects the most intelligence, the man or the woman? Take Adam and Eve, was it not the woman who first discovered that she was in error and was the first to admit it?" To me this was a new definition of intelligence, and I never lost sight of it. The result of her talk was indeed wonderful, for within a short time I began to have numerous calls to lecture, and, what is more, felt the inspiration of Truth to accept these fearlessly and to prove that a woman can declare the truth and heal the sick as well as a man.

On June 6, 1899, when Mrs. Eddy spoke in Tremont Temple, I was on the platform and had been asked to speak there, as I was a lecturer at that time. When Mrs. Eddy entered from the back of the platform we were all delighted, and the few words she spoke meant much to us. Lady Dunmore and her son Lord Fincastle were seated next to me.

I was among those who heard Mrs. Eddy speak from the balcony at Pleasant View in 1903. I also saw her in 1904 in front of the Concord church when she spoke a few words to Mr. Edward P. Bates, the President of The Mother Church, as she handed him a gavel to be used at the annual church meetings.

In June 1903 another change came in my own work, when I was called on Mrs. Eddy's recommendation to become one of the Editors of our periodicals.

A few months later I had the great privilege of another interview with Mrs. Eddy at Pleasant View, where I remained for a few days on her gracious invitation. Every minute spent in her presence meant so much because of her wonderful reflection of divine intelligence, and so I spoke very little, preferring to listen to her inspired words. One morning when I was a guest there she sent for me to come to her room on leaving the breakfast table, and when I entered it she said she wished to call my attention to a passage which she had just read, and which had come to her with new light. She opened the Bible and read from John 4:39–42, but laid the emphasis upon verse 42, which reads: "And said unto the woman, Now we believe, not because of thy saying: for we have heard him ourselves, and know that this is indeed the Christ, the Saviour of the world." She paused a moment and said, "I think I ought to call the other members of the household to receive this message," and this she did. As these students came into the room she repeated what she had said to me, and again read the verse mentioned. Looking very earnestly and lovingly at all of us she added, "You can each of you, I am sure, say this for yourselves, that you believe, not because of what I have told you, but because you have proved for yourselves that Christian Science is indeed 'the Christ, the Saviour of the world.' "

The Board of Directors and the Editors were summoned by telegram to meet Mrs. Eddy at Pleasant View at two o'clock in the afternoon of October 5, 1905. On our arrival we were shown to her study and took our seats in a semicircle in front of the chair where she usually sat, in the corner of the room. There were present Messrs. Chase, Johnson, Armstrong, Knapp, McLellan, Willis, and myself. After greeting us Mrs. Eddy addressed the Directors individually by name, and asked each one if he read carefully the *Journal* and *Sentinel*. Each one in turn said he did, but perhaps not so carefully as he ought to do. She then said quite gravely that she wanted them to read the periodicals with the utmost care, and to assist her in guarding them from any errone-ous or misleading statements which might escape the notice of the Editors.

She then took up from her desk a copy of the *Christian Science Sentinel* of September 30, 1905, and read these words from an arti-cle, "a diseased body is not acceptable to God." She read them without indicating in any way whether she approved or disap-proved of them, then asked each of us if we considered that state-ment scientific. I happened to be the last of that group of seven persons, and Mrs. Eddy again read the words already quoted, and asked me if I considered the statement scientific. I replied that I had stumbled over it twice, but had decided to let it go through. Mrs. Eddy paused for a moment and then said in tones I can never forget, "Then you are the one to blame. You are my stu-dent, are you not?" I responded, "Yes, Mrs. Eddy, I have that great privilege." She then said, "Did I ever teach you anything like this?" To this I made no response, beginning to realize that a serious mistake had been made. She then addressed the whole group and said in strong tones, "Now, will you any of you tell me whether God has any more use for a well body than for a sick one?" This came like a flash of light, and we all wondered at our own dullness. Turning to me again she said that her reason for having me come to Boston was because she hoped I would have been able to see that her teachings were strictly adhered to in the articles which went out, and that I had failed to do this in the statement in question. She insisted that man's likeness to God is never a physical likeness, and called our attention to page 313 of *Science and Health,* lines 12–19.

Then she turned to *Science and Health* and asked us to read daily for the present on page 295, lines 5–24. She turned to one of those present and said, "You sometimes believe, do you not, that you can see as well through a brick wall as through a window?" He respectfully replied that he hoped he did not, but she said it would sometimes appear as if he did because of what he wrote, and with her usual splendid dignity and yet great humility, she referred to herself as the transparency through which the light of Truth had come to our age, and speaking for myself I can only say that this means a thousand times more to me today, after the added years of experience, than it did when Mrs. Eddy talked with us.

Mrs. Eddy went on to speak of the work of Christ Jesus, and she said that she was sometimes troubled at the false concepts of the Master which occasionally found their way into the *Journal* and *Sentinel,* and turning to the Editors she said very forcefully, "I do not want to see any more of those namby-pamby concepts of Jesus go out through our periodicals to mislead people as to what he actually taught." She quoted some of his severe denunciations of the scribes and Pharisees, where he called them whited sepulchers, and so forth, and she added, "If I had said such severe things about those who have opposed Christian Science as he did to his opponents, I would have been put to death long ago."

Here it is only right to say that while I was deeply grieved to have caused our Leader disappointment, indeed sorrow, a rebuke from her was worth much more than the praise of others, and I took it gratefully. Mrs. Eddy talked with us for nearly two hours, and left it very clear that no one is to be judged by his or her physical condition, but by character and spiritual attainments.

Within a year of the time I became an Editor, I was also appointed by Mrs. Eddy a member of the Bible Lesson Committee, which work I enjoyed greatly, and I remained a member of this committee until 1918. I have always felt that one of the most important parts of our Leader's divinely inspired instruction for the advancement of our Cause was the selecting of subjects for the Lesson-Sermons, and thus providing for the spiritual needs of humanity beyond the present hour and into the far future. As the years go by I see this more and more.

In 1919 I was called to be a member of The Christian Science Board of Directors, and while I shrank from the responsibilities involved in this forward step, it seemed that obedience was the need of the hour, and I at once responded.

Our Leader as Teacher and Friend

FRANK WALTER GALE

*O*n a certain occasion our beloved Leader, Mary Baker Eddy, sent a message to a meeting of students, and one of the statements may well be applied to this gathering. It was: "You have convened only to convince yourselves of this grand verity: namely, the unity in Christian Science. Cherish steadfastly this fact. Adhere to the teachings of the Bible, Science and Health, and our Manual, and you will obey the law and gospel. Have one God and you will have no devil. Keep yourselves busy with divine Love" (*The First Church of Christ, Scientist, and Miscellany,* pp. 251–252).

In 1885 my mother had been confined to her bed for over three years, and when the doctors finally said they could do no more for her, Christian Science was brought to her attention through a newspaper article which told of the healing of one through mental and spiritual means. This appealed to my mother, and she asked me to find out more about it. A practitioner was found who called to see my mother and commenced treatment. At the end of a week she was up and walking around the house, and by the end of another week was entirely well. We immediately secured a copy of *Science and Health with Key to the Scriptures* by Mary Baker Eddy, and my mother and I took up its study.

In 1887 we moved from San Francisco to San Diego, California, where my mother and I introduced Christian Science and started the healing work there.

In 1888 I applied to Mrs. Eddy for class instruction and was accepted. I arrived in Boston a few days before the class convened, and went to the College at 571 Columbus Avenue to see if

Mrs. Eddy's residence at 385 Commonwealth Avenue, Boston, where she lived from December 1887 until May 1889

there were any letters for me, and also to see Mr. Frye, who was Mrs. Eddy's secretary at that time. I was told that Mr. Frye was over at 385 Commonwealth Avenue, so I went over there. And then I had my first greeting from Mrs. Eddy, and it was in this wise: Just as I got there, a man drove up to the house with some provisions, and rang the bell. While he was waiting for the door to open, I walked up the steps and stood at the side of the door. When the maid opened the door, the man asked if he should bring the things in the front way or how, and while they were talking Mrs. Eddy, who was in the hall, came to the door and told him to take the things around the back way.

As he turned to go down the steps, I stepped up to the door and said, "Excuse me, but I was looking for Mr. Frye." Mrs. Eddy replied that he was not in. I then ventured to ask if this was Mrs. Eddy, and when she said it was, I told her I was Frank Gale. When I told her who I was a look came into her eyes, as she shook hands with me, that I shall never forget. I cannot describe it, but it made me feel at home. Almost the first thing she asked me was if my mother was with me. When I told her frankly that my mother was anxious to come but we did not have the funds, she said she was sorry, that it would not have been so had she known. She then expressed the hope that my mother might come to the next class.

A few days later I had the blessed privilege of sitting in class, and the sunlight of Truth reflected in Mrs. Eddy's face made the cloudy days during class radiant with light. She was refinement itself. Words fail to describe her. She was so poised and dignified; and yet one felt such gentleness, humbleness, such meekness.

Mrs. Eddy asked questions of the students, going over the ground laid down in the chapter entitled "Recapitulation" in *Science and Health,* and of course brought in illustrations to help make it clear. There was one point that she stressed and made very positive. In order to heal quickly we must not recognize any disease in a patient, even as a belief, because we make more or less a reality of it when we do; but we should go to a patient with the feeling that he is well and we want to show him that he is well. She told us that when she had healed instantaneously she had lost sight of the personality and realized only the presence of the spiritual and perfect.

One day Mrs. Eddy allowed the class to ask most of the questions, and at the end of the session she announced that *she* was going to do the questioning at the next lesson, and we could prepare to be *sifted*. And she kept her promise. Her keen discernment enabled her to uncover the error in thought of any student, and she never hesitated to do it, but with much love and understanding.

I shall never forget the light that shone in her face when we considered the subject of Love. As nearly as I can recall her words, she made this statement: "God is Love; to love is to express God, and as God is eternal Life, if we always loved we should always express Life, and never have a belief of death. Hate is the opposite of Love, and leads to death; therefore never hate anything."

Shortly after I returned to San Diego, my mother and I started Sunday services, which later developed into the organization of First Church of Christ, Scientist, in that city.

Whenever I read the parable of the tares and wheat, or references to this parable by Mrs. Eddy, I am reminded of a letter she wrote to me in 1891, in which she said: "You are *growing*. The Father has sealed you, and the opening of these seals must not surprise you. The character of Christ is wrought out in our lives by just such processes. The tares and wheat appear to grow together until the harvest; then the tares are *first* gathered, that is, you have seasons of seeing your errors—and afterwards by reason of this very seeing, the tares are burned, the error is destroyed. Then you see Truth plainly and the wheat is 'gathered into barns,' it becomes permanent in the understanding."

And in this same letter she added: "The healing will grow more easy and be more immediate as you realize that God, good, *is all,* and good is Love. You must gain Love, and lose the false sense called love. You must feel the Love that *never* faileth,—that

90

perfect sense of divine power that makes healing no longer power but *grace*. Then you will have the Love that casts out fear and when fear is gone doubt is gone and your work is done. Why? because it never was *undone*."

For many years I came to Boston for the Annual Meetings, and on several occasions had interesting and instructive interviews with Mrs. Eddy.

You are all familiar with the picture of Mrs. Eddy as she stood on the balcony of her home at Pleasant View, June 29, 1903, and gave a brief address to the large gathering below (*Miscellany*, pp. 170–171). I assisted in directing the people and carriages as they arrived that morning, and in the afternoon I was in the group who eagerly listened to her every word.

It is ever a source of inspiration and courage to me when I reflect on Mrs. Eddy's untiring efforts on behalf of her students and the Cause of Christian Science. Most of the letters I received from her throughout the years were in her own handwriting. And how impersonally she turned us to her works. When a new edition of *Science and Health* was about to be published she wrote me: "I was pleased to hear from you. Had felt that our Father was giving you line upon line and you had the best Teacher and most loving in all His ways. This abated any care of mine for you.

"In reading my revised edition that is, by the way, published this week there is no special direction requisite. The general rule is to commence with the first chapter, read slowly and pause as you read to apply certain portions which meet your present need,—to thought that will carry them out in action. The book is complete in itself, it is a teacher and healer. Has 50 pages more than the old edition just past. The labor I have bestowed on it you cannot reckon, there are more signs of it than you can *see*, but not more than will be *felt*."

May we go forward conscious of the Love which heals—that irresistible, irrepressible, fervent desire to bless, and thereby be obedient to our Leader's admonition in *Miscellaneous Writings* (pp. 206–207): "As you journey, and betimes sigh for rest 'beside the still waters,' ponder this lesson of love. Learn its purpose; and in hope and faith, where heart meets heart reciprocally blest, drink with me the living waters of the spirit of my life-purpose,— to impress humanity with the genuine recognition of practical, operative Christian Science."

The Primary Class of 1889 and Other Memories

EMMA EASTON NEWMAN

Still vivid in memory is the picture of our loved Leader, Mary Baker Eddy, as she addressed the March Primary class of 1889. This class assembled on Monday, February 25, at 10 a.m., at 571 Columbus Avenue, in Boston, in the house which was known as the Massachusetts Metaphysical College. A limited number might board and room there during class, and my parents and I were happy to be among the number.

The class was held in a large room at the rear of the house. The sixty-five students were representative of our Cause at that time, coming from many parts of the United States and Canada. Some had already been taught by Mrs. Eddy in a Primary class; some had been through a Normal class; some had studied under qualified teachers, and others, like ourselves, had not studied under a teacher.

Our Leader's appearance at that time was of a woman many years younger than the recorded number. The hair was still dark, the eyes glowing with the inner fire of spiritual inspiration. The delicate complexion permitted her color to vary in response to her thought. The reproduced photograph used in the latest edition of *The Life of Mary Baker Eddy* by Sibyl Wilbur gives a good idea of her appearance at that period.

There could be incisiveness when occasion demanded. One member of the class, a retired minister inclined to controversy, asked Mrs. Eddy how, if people took cold mentally, his little two-year-old child could get cold by walking about with bare feet

93

when too young to be conscious of breaking a so-called material law. Mrs. Eddy vehemently replied, "You took cold for him." She asked one woman what she would do if she were treating a case that did not yield. The answer was, "I would examine my own thought." Mrs. Eddy then asked her what she would do if the case still did not yield. The woman answered she would handle animal magnetism. Again Mrs. Eddy repeated her question, and the woman said, "I suppose I'd give it up." "And that," Mrs. Eddy said, "is just what you should *not* do."

Of course no notes were tolerated, and she questioned each one individually. As a young girl I kept a diary, and on the second day of class is this entry: "Mrs. Eddy is wonderfully clear, and we are enjoying the class beyond anything we ever expected."

Her ready wit was well known to all who enjoyed her friendship or sat under her teaching. She was illustrating the point that "matter and mortal mind are one" (*Unity of Good,* p. 35), and that mortal mind is the only factor to be considered. She said, "It is like the man who said, 'My wife and I are one—and I am that one!' "

One day after announcing that the subject of that day's teaching would be animal magnetism, she said, "Today we will talk something up to talk it down." It impressed me deeply at the time, and the thought has remained with me that, for lucidity and brevity of statement regarding her teaching of that which claims to be power but in reality is not, these words are unsurpassed: "Today we will talk something up to talk it down."

We all have the benefit of our Leader's own résumé of this class in *Miscellaneous Writings.* Here she speaks of the autograph album in which we wrote our names. My father made the presentation, in response to which she said, "Among the gifts of my students, this of yours is one of the most beautiful and the most costly, because you have signed your names" (*ibid.,* p. 281). In emphasizing the necessity for unity among her followers she used solemn words. To quote again from the résumé (*ibid.,* p. 279), she said, "We, to-day, in this class-room, are enough to convert

94

the world if we are of one Mind; for then the whole world will feel the influence of this Mind." In view of present seeming world conditions, how intensified should be our prayer that we, her followers of today, may demonstrate that one Mind. We cannot question that a burdened world awaits our fulfillment of her promise and prophecy. The great and lasting imprint on memory left by our Leader's teaching in the two classes in which I had the privilege to be enrolled, as well as that received in private conversations, is the fact that, while erroneous situations may be considered and discussed, error must never be accepted as real; that error must never have the last word. Always she lifted one's thought to a higher level, and when so lifted she required that there should be no return to the discord.

Her choice of words in which to clothe her ideas in her classroom work was as distinctive and thought-arresting as in her writings. Miss M. Louise Baum, one-time Editor of The Home Forum page of *The Christian Science Monitor,* wrote: "In the writings of Mary Baker Eddy there is this great quality of spontaneous expression. There was somewhat to say that must get said. The freedom and power, the unconventionality and fearless handling of her tool to the end she sought are slowly vindicating themselves in the case of this great writer, and the world is beginning to admit that in the writings of the greatest woman Leader and organizer the world has ever seen is the enduring vitality of great literature. . . . It [her style] is beautiful and strong, and moves with a marvelous celerity to its point; yet it is so weighted with meaning that one may well lift every word as if it were a treasure casket. In this age when a certain smooth propriety of speech is reducing to deadly levels of commonplace countless pages of print Mrs. Eddy's writing stands out as individual as the brushwork of some medieval scribe and illuminator of the days before machine-made books. . . . There are no extra words to veil thought or to cover vacancy. She has achieved the great thing: her thinking stands forth in its naked sincerity as if she had done away with the medium of speech and had brought forth the

Word itself which is one with thought and deed. . . . She is herself what she says, she has lived it out, and so it is that her words live and kindle life in others." (From *The Christian Science Monitor,* March 3, 1911, International Edition.)

To follow Peter's counsel, "Use hospitality one to another without grudging" (I Peter 4:9), was no task to the mistress of Pleasant View. The cheer, daintiness, and order of the home radiated its owner's individuality. Above all, she gave of herself freely. In June 1893, during my father's pastorate of The Mother Church, The First Church of Christ, Scientist, in Boston, Massachusetts, we received an invitation written by her own hand, firm and character revealing as were all the letters we received from her. The invitation was to my parents and myself, and we were to arrive in the middle of the afternoon and remain overnight. With what joy we went you can well imagine. We were met at the station and driven to Pleasant View, where Mrs. Eddy received us almost immediately. We were with her practically all the time until eight in the evening, when she excused herself. I was struck by her loving manner towards those who served her. She addressed them usually as "dear," and they addressed her, lovingly, as "Mother." Even in ordinary conversation error was gently rebuked. Someone had spoken of a rather flagrant mistake some Scientist had made. She remarked on how easy it was to uncover *other* people's errors.

She was a remarkably good listener, but above all one realized that she listened to God; that she walked with her hand in God's hand. In a letter dated March 10, 1893, she had written to my father when he began his pastorate: "I found it essential, when the pastor of this church, to lead them by my own state of love and spirituality. By fervor in speaking the Word, by tenderness in searching into their needs—and specially by *feeling myself* and uttering the *spirit* of Christian Science—together with the letter." Her commendation produced the effect of causing one to see one's shortcomings and at the same time determine to overcome them. When she spoke of Christ Jesus, it seemed as if time and space, the barrier of two millenniums and two hemispheres, were swept away. She spoke at this time with ardor of her work on her illustrated poem, *Christ and Christmas.* It was evidently dear to her heart. The verse on page 39 of this poem shows our Leader's utter realization that the human self was not a factor in her writing, but, rather, that it was set aside that the revealed Science of Christianity might freely flow. This stanza reads as follows:

> "As in blest Palestina's hour,
>   So in our age,
> 'T is the same hand unfolds His power,
>   And writes the page."

The following morning of this visit we were called to breakfast about seven-thirty. Mrs. Eddy greeted us and sat at the head of her table, but she explained that she had breakfasted much earlier and that she would talk while we ate. Again she gave us generously of her time until our departure, about eleven o'clock. It was like class teaching all over again, and impressions deeper than words remained and governed thought. On leaving Pleasant View we drove through Concord and on a few miles to Boscawen to call on my grandfather's cousin, Bartlett Corser. For the first time we heard with great interest from him of his father's and his own intimate friendship with the Baker family, his father being the Rev. Enoch Corser spoken of by our Leader (*Retrospection and Introspection,* p. 14; *Message to The Mother Church for 1901,* p. 32). Cousin Bartlett was about three years older than Mrs. Eddy, and his memories of her girlhood were beautiful and distinct. Much of this has been recorded in Sibyl Wilbur's biography of our Leader (pp. 31–33). On our return to Boston my mother wrote to Mrs. Eddy of our deep gratitude for the precious hours spent with her, and also told of the call on the cousin and of his treasured memories of her and her home and family. Immediately a reply, dated July 2, 1893, was received which contained this paragraph: "Your letter was an oasis. It was like lying down in green pastures beside *still* waters. . . . Nothing could have given me more pleasure, that pertains to earth, than your account of seeing Mr. Bartlett Corser and of his relationship! I remember him as an ideal man, a scholar, a great hearted and great minded man. And his father, Rev. Enoch Corser, I used to think was the most *naturally* eloquent gifted preacher I ever heard speak. It was the sweet memory of girlhood days that your letter awakened which rested me. Thank you for it. I shall certainly try to have him visit me." A few months later Mrs. Eddy wrote a lovely expression of her thanks to my father for a sermon of his which was published in the *Journal* of October 1893. It read: "God bless you and every day show you a little more of *Infinite Love*. Just your daily bread, more you will not digest."

On the twenty-seventh of December 1895, came the invitation to New Year's luncheon, with the admonition not to speak to anyone about it until it was consummated—a very usual request from her. We were no sooner ushered into the living room at the left of the entrance hallway than we heard a light, swift step on the stairs, and Mrs. Eddy was taking her guests by the hand and saying, "How good God is to give me this pleasure!" We hardly knew what to say, because we were so conscious of God's goodness to us in permitting us to be there. She explained that she so often had to see people for some specific reason, but that we were "just company."

During the visit she said there were things she wanted to tell her church, and that she should come again soon. The fulfillment of this promise was her delivery of the Communion Address in the same month—January 1896. (*Miscellaneous Writings,* p. 120.) In referring to her first time of addressing us in The Mother Church, May 26, 1895, she said, "I discerned every mentality there, but saw no personality." This gave us an enlarged and wonderful sense of what spiritual discernment was, in contrast with the earth-weighted sense of personality. At the table there were five guests, besides the beloved hostess and members of the household. Mrs. Eddy keenly enjoyed a story which illustrated mortal mind's absurdity. Someone told a story of two men in a hotel room. One wanted air and the other did not. Finally, the one wanting air got up, and failing in the dark to open a window broke a pane of glass. Then he could sleep comfortably, but the other man took cold. In the morning it turned out that he had broken a pane of glass in a bookcase!

We were telling her of some of the splendid healings reported at the testimony meetings, and she was listening eagerly, as she always did to any demonstration of the healing power of the Christ, Truth. I said, "Oh, Mother, you should be there to hear them." She smiled so sweetly, and said that she wished that she might. One realized that her retirement from public life in Boston came just at the time the persecutions were lessening, but that had she stayed to enjoy these fruits of her labors she might not have gone on to higher heights of demonstration and worked out the God-ordained plan by which what she called the "stately goings of Christian Science" (*Miscellaneous Writings,* p. 245) would be forwarded.

On the afternoon of November 19, 1898, I received a telegram reading, "Be at Christian Science Hall at Concord tomorrow afternoon at 4:00" (signed) "M. B. Eddy." In response to similar calls many of us took the train from Boston for Concord that evening. We were all very happy to be called, but distinctly human in our speculation as to the reason for the call. The personnel of this class was much like that of the March class in 1889, except that, indicative of the growth in our movement, there were those from greater distances. England, Scotland, Canada, and our Far West were well represented. Those at greater distances were, of course, notified in time to make the journey. One of the definite memories is the loving way in which she spoke of children. She said that she loved them, that theirs was the white unwritten page, and that it was because of her love for them that they came to greet her as she went on her daily drive. There was the time when she called for a volunteer to read Luke's account of the resurrection. We were all silent until a young man said, "I will,

Christian Science Hall, Concord, New Hampshire

Mother." She said he was her Nathaniel, always ready. She asked us, each one, how we would heal a case of sickness. She listened lovingly and patiently, but she seemed disappointed that more was not said about the healing power of Love, and then she gave us her answer in words which lifted us to a higher vision of what Christian healing really was.

In reviewing the life of the Discoverer and Founder of Christian Science, one sees that dissatisfaction with scholastic theology only drove her closer to God and the revelation of Christ Jesus. Instead of forsaking the Bible, she searched it more diligently, looking for the vital spark which had kept its teachings intact in spite of persecution, skepticism, human philosophies, and counterfeit presentations of Christianity. She lived the Christly teachings in unselfed labors for family and friends, in working for temperance reform, emancipation of the slaves, and higher education for women, until these gleams of light merged into the glory of revealed scientific Christianity. Mary of old said, "Rabboni; which is to say, Master" (John 20:16). Mary of our day said (*Retrospection and Introspection,* p. 23): "When the door opened, I was waiting and watching; and, lo, the bridegroom came! The character of the Christ was illuminated by the midnight torches of Spirit. My heart knew its Redeemer."

The Discoverer and Founder of Christian Science

ANNIE LOUISE ROBERTSON

*I*t is a joy as well as a privilege to have the opportunity of speaking about our beloved Leader, Mary Baker Eddy, to a large body of appreciative listeners who also love and revere her.

In *The First Church of Christ, Scientist, and Miscellany* (p. 120), Mrs. Eddy says, "Those who look for me in person, or elsewhere than in my writings, lose me instead of find me." However, it is natural that those who have so marvelously benefited by her writings should love to hear of the human character of our revered Leader; and we who have had the unspeakable privilege of seeing and talking with her, love to recall how uplifting the experiences were, and gladly share them.

It is valuable to have even a slight knowledge of the wonderful way in which the Discoverer and Founder of Christian Science established our Cause on a firm foundation, correcting where correction was needed, and never failing to encourage and inspire the workers, thereby in every way proving her spiritual leadership.

Mrs. Eddy admonishes us in the Christian Science textbook, *Science and Health with Key to the Scriptures,* that the "goal is never reached while we hate our neighbor or entertain a false estimate of anyone whom God has appointed to voice His Word" (p. 560). Now if we would share with our Leader the revelation that God gave to her, and which she has imparted so generously to others, it is important that we understand some of the human footsteps which led to the present prosperity and stability of our Cause, and at least catch a glimpse of her true womanhood.

Sometimes a healing has been delayed because of a misunderstanding of our Leader's character; and on the other hand, often a great victory has been won through a sincere appreciation of her service to humanity.

Some of us remember the days when a small congregation, at first less than four hundred people, met each Sunday in what was then called Chickering Hall on Tremont Street, in Boston—an earnest, sincere group striving to re-form their lives into the new way of thinking, living, and healing the sick.

As the congregation at Chickering Hall increased it became necessary to move into a larger hall; but soon this, too, was inadequate to accommodate the ever-increasing congregation. So the students wanted to build a church; but Mrs. Eddy waited until they were prepared to take the responsibility which necessarily would fall upon their shoulders; and under her guidance the Original Edifice of The Mother Church was built.

As the true idea of Church grew clearer and stronger, the congregation soon more than filled the auditorium; and in 1898, our Leader, awake and alert, gave the order to form branch churches in the vicinity of Boston. Soon, however, still more room was necessary, as the attendance was rapidly increasing; and the students were most eager to build a larger church. Again Mrs. Eddy waited for them to be wise enough to meet and overcome the antagonism which would arise as the prosperity of the Cause became more apparent; in 1902 she consented to the building of the Extension of The Mother Church. This was a great undertaking, requiring much devotion and sacrifice on the part of the students throughout the Field; and Mrs. Eddy's faith in divine guidance always stood out like a beacon light above the turmoil of mortal existence.

At one time it seemed difficult to find Christian Scientists who were competent to fill the pulpits of the growing churches; and while the church members talked over the matter and worried about it, Mrs. Eddy said little. However, at the right moment she knew just what to do; she appointed two Readers, and ordained the Bible and *Science and Health with Key to the Scriptures* as our Pastor.

While our Leader always waited patiently for the right time in which to adopt some new and more spiritual method, when it was once decided she brooked no delay; and her living faith always brought its reward.

Christian Scientists owe much gratitude to the little band of workers who loyally and unhesitatingly followed and obeyed our Leader in those early endeavors to prove the teachings of Christ Jesus in healing the sick and destroying sin.

We have a vivid recollection of the joy that came to these earlier workers when for the first time an opportunity was given Christian Scientists to become members of The Mother Church. With what eagerness we sought the way in which we could take this step! This was in Chickering Hall in 1892 and 1893. It seemed to the workers then, as it does now, a wonderful privilege to be able to become a member of the Church of Christ, Scientist.

It was always inspiring to witness the matchless courage and unfailing patience with which Mrs. Eddy guided the formation of the human organization of the Church of Christ, Scientist. It certainly required a strong spiritual conviction to face the opposition from many of the ecclesiastical world, reversing as she did many old methods of ritual service.

As we recall the time when our Leader took an active part in the government of this movement, we do not forget that repeatedly there were errors to be overcome; yet it was a joyous time, for the triumph of truth over error stands out above all as a rainbow above the clouds.

Mrs. Eddy in the Original Mother Church

There will be some here who may remember the time, May 26, 1895, when Mrs. Eddy preached in the Original Mother Church.

On this occasion she came down from Concord and passed the night in the room which was called "Mother's Room," in the tower of the Original Mother Church edifice. There were only a few church members who knew of her presence in the church— the Directors, the Readers, and two or three others.

Mrs. Eddy did not decide until the very last moment whether or not she should preach. So she requested the Readers to proceed as usual with the Sunday lesson, and in case she decided to preach she would enter the auditorium and come down to the pulpit. A member of the choir was appointed to watch the door at which she would enter and notify the organist to play, which would signify to the Readers that Mrs. Eddy was coming.

The door did open, and our Leader stood there a moment or two as if in prayer; and then, lifting her head quickly, she walked down the aisle with her usual light, quick step. As soon as she came forward, the organist began to play, the choir rose, and immediately the entire congregation rose. As Mrs. Eddy came down the aisle she turned her gaze toward the congregation, but far above it, as one inspired, apparently unconscious of the audience.

The First Reader came down to meet her at the foot of the steps leading to the platform, and escorted her to a chair that had been provided for her. She sat quietly listening to a solo, and then arose and gave the uplifting address, an extract from which will be found on page 106 of *Miscellaneous Writings*. Her voice, without effort, had the most unusual carrying power. This was clearly proved later when she spoke at an Annual Meeting of her church held on June 6, 1899, in Tremont Temple, in Boston.

There were many cases of physical healing in the little church that morning, and many more experienced a change of heart. A friend who had persistently clung to an unreasonable dislike for Mrs. Eddy, told me that as Mrs. Eddy was coming down the aisle she turned and looked into her face, and the resistance melted away completely, her eyes filled with tears, and after that she was absolutely loyal to our Leader. There were many other similar experiences which I heard of at the time.

When Mrs. Eddy was residing in Lynn, also while she lived in Boston, one constantly heard of many cases of healing which she accomplished; and in every one that I heard about the healing was instantaneous. A well-known case was the healing of a man who had been deaf and dumb. For many years afterwards he was at The Mother Church services and often gave testimonies. There is no doubt that much of Mrs. Eddy's healing work has never been recorded.

In speaking of so remarkable a character, of one who had so spiritual a vision, it is impossible to portray it fully. It is simply incomparable—above human praise or criticism, for there are no words that can express what the whole world owes to such a consecrated life.

She was the most consistent follower of the teachings of Christ Jesus that the world has ever known. She, too, reflected the immortal courage that dared to face the whole world and tell it that it was wrong. When Mrs. Eddy talked about the Cause, which she invariably did, it was easy to realize that we were living in a time like that of the early Christians.

Mrs. Eddy had a quiet, most gracious manner, with an entire lack of self-assertiveness that was most unusual. To be in her presence was an inspiration never to be forgotten. In the early days the students loved to speak of her as "Mother."

The Church of Christ, Scientist, is a living memorial to our great Leader and teacher. Each day it is speaking louder and clearer of the healing message of the Christ, Truth, which she brought to the world.

It would be a great danger to our Cause if Christian Scientists should fail to keep alive the memory of, and gratitude for, the life and sacrifices of our great Leader.

And as we have seen our beloved Leader, Mary Baker Eddy, dedicate her life to the Cause of Christian Science, so now it remains for her followers to consecrate and dedicate their lives to carrying on the great work which she has given into their hands.

The Call to Concord

GEORGE WENDELL ADAMS

When I received the unexpected call to attend the last class of our beloved Leader, Mary Baker Eddy, in Concord, New Hampshire, I had been in the active practice of Christian Science for about three years. Previously, I had received class instruction from one of Mrs. Eddy's students and had reached my decision to enter the practice while attending the Massachusetts Institute of Technology. Perhaps it should be stated here that I had become a member of The Mother Church in July 1893, two years following my first interest in Christian Science.

The young man with whom I shared my practitioner's office also received a call from Mrs. Eddy to be in Christian Science Hall at four o'clock on Sunday afternoon, November 20, 1898. The invitations came on short notice, and there was nothing in them to indicate what was to take place. My request came by letter and my friend's came by telegram. Both invitations were marked "confidential," so that neither of us knew at that time that the other one had been called to attend the class.

Saturday morning, November 19, the day we were to leave Boston, my friend asked me if he might borrow my suitcase. I said I was sorry but I expected to use it myself. He did not tell me why he needed it, and naturally I did not reveal to him my reason for its use. The matter was settled amicably and, later that day to our surprise, we met at the North Station in Boston and boarded the same train for Concord.

On reaching the Eagle Hotel in Concord, we saw many familiar faces. None of us knew what was to take place, and we did not discuss it because of our confidential invitations. Later we found that Mrs. Eddy's reason for observing strict secrecy about this class was to avoid the stir that might be occasioned by the many others who desired to share the great opportunity but whom she could not accommodate at that time.

Sunday morning we attended services in Christian Science Hall, which was on the site of the present edifice. Mr. Ezra M. Buswell, the First Reader, read as part of his scriptural reading: "After these things the Lord appointed other seventy also. . . ." (Luke 10:1). This gave us our first inkling of the reason for our presence in Concord.

That afternoon each one was in his place before the appointed time. There were editors, lecturers, former doctors, lawyers, and businessmen in the class. Promptly at four o'clock our Leader entered the hall escorted by her long-time secretary, Calvin Frye. The members of the class stood up as she walked quickly and gracefully to the platform and took her place. She was vigorous and vivid and appeared much younger than her years, but there was also great meekness and holiness in her bearing. One never could forget her heavenly expression as she looked searchingly into the face of each one as he stood in response to the roll call. Well we knew that this experience would indeed impart a fresh impetus to higher spiritual attainments.

Our instruction started with God and was followed by man. One of the outstanding things in the teaching of this class was the time given by Mrs. Eddy in her endeavor to impress upon us that there is but one God; and consequently but one full reflection,—the compound idea, man. She indicated that only as her students grasp the fundamental fact that one God could have but one full reflection, did they have the basic sense of Christian Science and the scientific starting point.

This instruction in no way conflicted with Mrs. Eddy's teaching as given in her textbook relative to individual man and ideas. Here she states in effect that Jesus' declaration, "I and my Father are one," means "one in quality, not in quantity" (*Science and Health,* p. 361). She further amplifies this in these words: "There is but one creator and one creation. This creation consists of the unfolding of spiritual ideas and their identities, which are embraced in the infinite Mind and forever reflected. These ideas range from the infinitesimal to infinity, and the highest ideas are the sons and daughters of God" (*Science and Health,* pp. 502–503).

As her wonderful teaching on this subject unfolded to us with crystal clarity, we realized more fully than ever before that "God is indivisible. A portion of God could not enter man; neither could God's fulness be reflected by a single man, else God would be manifestly finite, lose the deific character, and become less than God. Allness is the measure of the infinite, and nothing less can express God" (*Science and Health,* p. 336). Nothing that Mrs. Eddy said would limit individual man from fully expressing God's qualities and the individual God-given ability to comprehend all that is real.

Our teacher's method was by questions and answers. Some of the members were asked to tell what the term God meant to them. The answers differed but all pointed to the infinite oneness of divine Principle. If one hesitated in his reply, the encouraging word was spoken, but there was no doubt but that she expected each one to speak distinctly and loud enough to be heard.

Mrs. Eddy said there were times in teaching when the deep things of Christian Science were being considered that the mesmeric sense of too continuous seriousness must be broken. She illustrated this in her teaching of this class by telling several amusing stories.

I recall one story in particular which she used to illustrate human philosophy. She said there once was a man who had a fox. He made a hole in the door of his house and stuck the tail of the fox through it from the inside. Very shortly a crowd had gathered outside and he went out to ask why they were there. The reply was that they were trying to figure out how the fox was able to get through such a small hole. This, said Mrs. Eddy, was human philosophy, always trying to figure out things that never happened.

Mrs. Eddy clearly showed us that to heal the sick, more and more weight must be cast on the side of Spirit. Instantaneous healings were accomplished through divine Love. To live love, to manifest the very presence of Love, would heal everything. It would raise the dead.

We glimpsed as never before the true import of the Decalogue and the Sermon on the Mount. No two days were ever filled with such practical instruction and heavenly inspiration. We had been blessed beyond words by the spiritual awakening which was ours as the result of our teacher's explanation of divine Principle. Several members of the class rose to their feet and humbly paid grateful tribute to the one whom God had "appointed to voice His Word." Indeed these loving tributes were timely expressions of our "correct sense" of divine Principle's "highest visible idea" (*Science and Health,* p. 560).

As the class drew to a close, we became more and more cognizant of our true heritage that "now are we the sons of God" (I John 3:2).

At parting, as we clasped Mrs. Eddy's hand and looked into her beloved face, we knew she had shared with us "God's most tender mercies" (*Poems,* p. 38).

Recollections of Mary Baker Eddy

JOHN C. LATHROP

*M*rs. Eddy writes in *Science and Health with Key to the Scriptures* (p. 25), "The divinity of the Christ was made manifest in the humanity of Jesus," and she also states that "without a correct sense of its highest visible idea, we can never understand the divine Principle" (*ibid.*, p. 560).

During the year 1896 I entered the practice of Christian Science, and shortly afterwards I first met Mrs. Eddy at her home at Pleasant View, Concord, New Hampshire. Her tender, motherly, human reception of a young man, who had just launched out into the deep, and cast his net on the right side of the ship, combined with her remarkable display of intelligence, poise, and love, impressed him deeply with her divine calling and impersonal leadership. After that sweet initiation into Mrs. Eddy's spiritual point of view, the way to me seemed more straight and positive than ever. Two years later I had the great privilege of sitting in Mrs. Eddy's last class, and five years after that of being called by her to join her household at Pleasant View and of witnessing firsthand Mrs. Eddy's human exemplification of Christian Science.

During the eighteen months I was a member of Mrs. Eddy's household, extending over a period of five years, to my knowledge she never remained in bed a single day because of incapacity. As a corresponding secretary I possessed every opportunity of observing our Leader, seeing and talking with her almost daily. Mrs. Eddy's demonstration of energy and activity was highly consistent. Her household was kept continually busy executing the work laid out for them by her.

Pleasant View, Concord, New Hampshire

There is perhaps no better way of indicating our Leader's faith in the healing Word of the Scriptures than was illustrated one night when her need seemed extreme. She turned to her Bible, and, as I have seen her frequently do, opened it at random. Governed by divine intelligence she opened the book to the thirteenth chapter of I Corinthians and read these words: "[Love] . . . beareth all things, believeth all things, hopeth all things, endureth all things." The next morning when she appeared at her desk, bright and well as usual, she told us that, when she read those healing words, she realized that she did not have to bear burdens, that Love bore them all, and she said that then the mesmerism broke and she felt free.

Mrs. Eddy was very methodical, very orderly about everything. She never procrastinated. She never put off till tomorrow the work she could do today. She did it *now,* and expected her followers to do the same. One day she called me to her study and asked me if I was doing my work. I replied, "I am trying to do it, Mother." She repeated her question. I replied as before, and attempted to explain. She said, "Stop, stop!" and gave me one of her penetrating looks which went right through one. "I asked you if you were doing what I gave you to do. You replied, 'I am trying to do it.' Now you are either doing a thing or you are not doing it. Were you doing it?" "No, Mother, I was not doing it," I replied. She said quickly, "When are you going to do it?" "Now," I replied. "Let me see you do it now," she said sternly. I returned to my room. I knew that if I did not do the required mental work now, I would soon be taking a train to my home. The rebuke to mortal mind, to the errors of "self-will, self-justification, and self-love" (*Science and Health,* p. 242), had been emphatic and merited, and presently a clear spiritual realization was obtained. At that moment my bell rang. Mrs. Eddy wanted me. I went to her calmly and found her smiling, sweet, and pleasant. The error had been destroyed. She did not refer to it again, but gave me more work to do.

One day Mrs. Eddy called the workers to her. Their mental work seemingly had been ineffective and depressing. She said in effect: Never become discouraged, dear ones. This work is not humdrum, it is growth. It is repeating and defeating, repeating and defeating, repeating and defeating. Is not this the way a mathematician becomes a mathematician? Another time, as I recall, she said, Humility is the door, honesty the way, and spirituality the summit.

One morning when we were assembled at 8:30 in Mrs. Eddy's study for the usual morning "conversation," one of the household asked her what she thought of the attempt on the part of some Readers in our churches to impersonalize their reading by reading in a monotone. Monotone? she asked. What do you mean? Is it reading such as I once heard when my hymn "Feed My Sheep" was read without expression or emphasis in such a way that I did not recognize it? Is that what you call impersonal reading? Then one said, Won't you read to us your hymn, Mother? At first she hesitated, then smiled, and taking up her book she read aloud to us that wonderful hymn. How I wish the radio had then been discovered, and her reading of this hymn could have gone out to the world! It was beautiful, so full of toneful expression and inflection; and such was her spiritual understanding that we never once thought of her personality; and when she reverently finished with "Shepherd, wash them clean," we felt we had had a baptism in Spirit, and were cleansed of much personal sense, self-consciousness, and fear.

Mrs. Eddy had remarkable eyes, deep and soulful. They seemed to look right through one into the distance, and similarly, when one looked into her keen, deep-set gray eyes, one seemed to look beyond the physical. Mrs. Eddy was light and graceful on her feet, and carried herself with a dignified and queenly bearing. She was outstanding and upstanding, straight and strong, though slight in stature, and about medium height. She was versatile, and always knew just how to approach a person, never forcing the thought with Christian Science, but would present the truth at the right time or not mention it at all.

All are familiar with her balcony picture, which I consider the best picture of her that we have. At the time of the gathering of Christian Scientists at Pleasant View in June 1903, Mr. Kimball, the Concord photographer, asked to photograph Mrs. Eddy on the balcony. At first she declined, but afterwards said, if he would stand at a distance and not distract the visitors, he might take the photograph. This he did, and that was when the good likeness of our Leader known as the balcony photograph was taken. The small negative was enlarged. Just before the time arrived for her to go out on the balcony to give her address, as a corresponding secretary I entered her room to ask her a question. She invited me to remain in the room and listen to the address through the open window. She then called her maid to put on her wrap and bonnet. It was raining a little, but this ceased when she went out. A multitude of joyous, upturned faces greeted their dear Leader in a stillness indescribable. She started right in and delivered her brief address slowly and distinctly. I was afterwards informed that every word was heard, so clear was her enunciation. She returned to her room and entered, her face radiantly happy. The maid removed her wrap and bonnet and she sat down in her big chair, folded her hands, and said to me, "Wasn't it a wonderful occasion?" Then she asked me, "What are they doing?" I looked below and told her they were having silent prayer. "We will pray, too," she said. "Now what are they doing?" she asked. "They are singing your hymn 'Shepherd,' Mother." After that they repeated "the scientific statement of being" (*Science and Health,* p. 468). Then they quietly dispersed; and when I told her, she said, "Now I will see what God says about it." She took up her Bible and opened it at random to read the first passage her eyes would light upon. It was Isaiah, thirty-fifth chapter, tenth verse: "And the ransomed of the Lord shall return, and come to Zion with songs and everlasting joy upon their heads: they shall obtain joy and gladness, and sorrow and sighing shall flee away." "See," she said, "how God is always with me. That verse I will add to my address." And this will explain how this Scripture appears at the end of her address (*The First Church of Christ, Scientist, and Miscellany,* p. 171), when she did not deliver it from the balcony. Then she said, "Now I will take my drive," which she did; and she drove through a big lane of hundreds of her happy followers, most of whom saw her near at hand for the first and only time.

Mrs. Eddy had a very keen wit. She could tell a story or a joke better than anyone I ever knew. I recall an episode, the finish of which was funny. For two years Mrs. Eddy was the honored guest of the City of Concord at its annual autumn State Fair. I remember on one occasion she graciously accepted the yearly invitation and drove around to the fairgrounds at two in the afternoon. She was happily received as she slowly circled the track. She bowed right and left, and seemed to enjoy greatly seeing again her old New Hampshire friends. An interesting incident occurred. Mrs. Eddy asked to witness the exhibition of high diving, and so her carriage drove through to the side of the pool of water where the diver, dressed as Mephistopheles, in red and with tail, was to dive down from a height through a hoop of fire into a small pool of water. Mrs. Eddy had told Judge and Mrs. Hanna, who accompanied her in her carriage, that she looked upon the exhibition as an example of overcoming fear, and she wanted to see it. The moment arrived, and the diver from his lofty height poised and gracefully dived downward through the fiery circle into the water, coming quickly to the surface. He walked out and up to Mrs. Eddy's carriage, bowed low to her and ran off. Mrs. Eddy had invited the First Members of The Mother Church to be present, and most of us were so intent watching her keen interest and pleasure that we missed the actual dive. When the man in red disappeared, Mrs. Eddy turned to Judge and Mrs. Hanna and said, "I beheld Satan as lightning fall from heaven."

The day Mrs. Eddy moved from Pleasant View to Chestnut Hill was beautiful, calm, and glorious. On that day, January 26, 1908, Mrs. Eddy went for her usual drive in Concord. In the meantime her household boarded the train of two cars. All the arrangements were made by Mrs. Eddy. Instead of returning to Pleasant View, she drove to the station and boarded her special car, one of the two. The news spread like wildfire. People scurried. Reporters tried to board the train, but were gently brushed off. Where was Mrs. Eddy going? Was she leaving Concord? were the questions asked. The reporters hastened to telephone to Boston, but just such an emergency had been foreseen by Mrs. Eddy. Arrangements had been made to detour on the Boston and Albany tracks just before reaching Boston. So Mrs. Eddy arrived at the Chestnut Hill Station, instead of at the Boston North Station, thus avoiding many who had congregated at the North Station to see her arrive. At the Chestnut Hill Station, carriages awaited her and her party, and within a few minutes she was in her new quarters in her commodious and beautiful new home. And such was her wisdom never to divulge her plans beforehand, that not a single person, except the few concerned, knew of this momentous move. My mother in New York City had had no inkling of it, and received her first news of the event from the newspapers the following morning.

Mrs. Eddy abhorred all hypocrisy, self-justification, or any excusing of error. She once said she could not teach a person who excused error, who closed his eyes to evil, that that person was not teachable. Someone sent her a set of the three little brass monkeys—"See no evil, hear no evil, speak no evil." That, said Mrs. Eddy in substance, is not Christian Science, it is heathen philosophy. Christian Scientists do not close their eyes to evil, but open them. They open their eyes, spiritual discernment, and awaken to the true nature of evil or sin, to its false claims, methods, subtlety, etc., and then realize its nothingness, its utter powerlessness to control or to harm.

Addendum

The following are sayings of Mrs. Eddy's at various times between 1903 and 1908, which, immediately on returning to my desk, I noted down to the best of my recollection. Other members of the household at the time confirmed these notes as substantially correct.

Every By-Law in the *Manual* is inspired. I did not write them any more than I wrote *Science and Health* [showing that both came to her through revelation]. I study *Science and Health* constantly.

Teach your students, patients, and everyone, to be loyal to the By-Laws, and they will be blessed.

Now measure yourself and your growth by your works, not by your words. All I have ever accomplished has been done by getting Mary out of the way, and letting God be reflected. When I would reach this tone, the sick would be healed without a word.

Don't be satisfied with one victory. Add victory upon victory.

The Writings of Mary Baker Eddy

DAISETTE D. S. McKENZIE

Christian Science is not something apart from this world, although it is apart from worldliness. It is the way to live. The disciples were not called Christians for many years. The teachings of Jesus were called simply "The Way." This characterization might well be applied to Christian Science in its profound simplicity. It is the way to live. Christian Scientists are not trying to draw converts out of the world to add one more to the sects already in existence. They seek to permeate the human mind with the true way to live, which restores the healing of early Christianity, enriches the affections and intellect, clearing the vision to behold something of the wonders that God hath prepared—wonders which cause us to exclaim, "O world invisible, we see thee." The student learns how his body may become obedient to Mind, how poverty may be banished through balancing his account with God, how he may retain his peace in the midst of discord, how it becomes possible to break the fetters of sickness and sin in the degree of his obedience to God. Is this not truly the way to live?

In a letter written in 1899, our Leader wrote: "All the people need, in order to love and adopt Christian Science, is the true sense of its Founder. In proportion as they have it, will our Cause advance." Some have believed that our Leader had, to some degree, relinquished her leadership of our movement, but instead her leadership rises today more grandly than ever. Christian Scientists are adding to the reverent appellation, "Our Leader," the grander concept of her spiritual leadership of the world. Through the discovery of Christian Science, God is today proclaiming His own government of the universe, and in resistance to this sublime government we hear one human voice after another crying, "No, *I* shall rule the world." This clamor will cease, and out of the fire shall emerge a purified consciousness more ready to learn the way to live. Our Leader encourages us to seek and find her in her writings. The hostility of mortal mind endeavors to separate her from her writings and so keep us from more intimate communion with her. Perhaps we sometimes read *Science and Health* without a thought of the author. May we not rather realize that we are not only reading the word of God, but that our communion with Him is through the message written by His chosen scribe? Also, in turning our thought to our Leader's other writings, when we seek the teaching contained in her Prose Works, is it not heartwarming to know that she is herself instructing us on practically every subject and situation in life, just as truly as though we sat in her classroom? We may still feel her vital interest in each one of us which we always felt when looking into her face and feeling the warm clasp of her hand.

How shall we attain unto sufficient thankfulness that we have with us these priceless writings, that we are not limited as were the early Christians in the possession of the written word? St. John twice records the lack of more comprehensive writings, implying a regret that all Christians have deeply felt. He says that if the many other things which Jesus did had been written, the world itself could not contain the volumes that should be written. Happily, today all is plainly written for our learning. It must, however, be regretfully acknowledged that there is a world of beauty and wonder in the life of Mary Baker Eddy which is not recorded, and can never be. Even the written word is known to us only in the degree of our spiritual advance. Our teacher has given us ample explanation as to the origin of her writings. She says (*The First Church of Christ, Scientist, and Miscellany,* p. 115), "I should blush to write of 'Science and Health with Key to the Scriptures' as I have, were it of human origin, and were I, apart from God, its author."

On one occasion, when we were visiting with our Leader, she

asked if we had seen a painting which was then in her room in the Original Church. It pictures a chair in which she sat when writing our textbook. Several sheets of manuscript were thrown on the floor beside it. "The picture is true to life," said Mrs. Eddy. "When the ideas of Truth poured into my thought, I was so careful not to miss anything, that I let my papers fall to the floor. When the moment of revelation passed, I gathered them up and arranged them." In her Prose Works she relates an interesting fact (*Miscellany,* p. 114): "I could not write these notes after sunset. All thoughts in the line of Scriptural interpretation would leave me until the rising of the sun. Then the influx of divine interpretation would pour in upon my spiritual sense as gloriously as the sunlight on the material senses. It was not myself, but the divine power of Truth and Love, infinitely above me, which dictated 'Science and Health with Key to the Scriptures.'" The prophecy of the Apocalypse was fulfilled—a woman had brought forth a child who was to rule all nations with a rod of iron, unchanging Principle. From that time on she labored to array the child in fine raiment, to clothe the idea in language befitting its divine origin. In her revisions of *Science and Health,* Mrs. Eddy studied with the utmost care every word of the text, and in a subsequent conversation she remarked that she often studied for months the origin and meaning of one word and its synonyms, before giving it a permanent place in the textbook, and in one notable instance she prayed and waited on God concerning a single word for three years. In thinking of this we may remind ourselves of the need for quoting her writings with correctness. Literary men and women in many lands have paid tribute to the quality of our Leader's writings.

When traveling in Switzerland many years ago, I met a distinguished clergyman in charge of an American church. In talking with him, I found him very hostile to Christian Science, especially to the work of healing. After some heated remarks on his part, he turned to a building which was being erected across the street from our hotel, and exclaimed: "Do you see those men on top of that fifty-foot wall? If they should fall they would be gone and nothing could be done about it." The next day my family attended the service in the Episcopal church of which he was rector. When he started to read the lesson appointed for that day, we were surprised and deeply interested to find that it was the account of the young man Eutychus, who fell from the third loft and was taken up dead, and who was restored by St. Paul. It seemed to us a message to the preacher from divine Love, for later he changed his view of Christian Science completely. Three years later, in 1893, at the World's Parliament of Religions in Chicago, we again met this clergyman as he came from the crowded hall where he had been listening to a message sent by our Leader. He greeted me cordially and spoke with appreciation of the service he had just attended, adding, "No one is educated today who has not read and pondered the writings of Mary Baker Eddy."

In support of this judgment is the following from a book entitled *A Plea for Christian Science* by an English author, Charles Herman Lea: "It will . . . be generally admitted that the true test of all books is the influence they have upon the lives and conduct of their readers. Judged by this standard, Mrs. Eddy's writings must be given a very high place indeed, for probably no other woman, either of this or of any previous age, has so powerfully influenced the world's thought and the lives of so many of its people."

A further example of the esteem in which her literary work is held, is the quotation from a prominent daily paper referring to the writings of Mary Baker Eddy: "The profound scholarship . . . that had penetrated the depths of the labyrinth of human knowledge may be accorded belated recognition. Men of letters . . . read the book which in the artistry of its proportion, the felicity of its expression, the puissance of its logic, its rare grammatical purity, the splendor of its visions, and the sweetness of its message is, in simple truth, a book of books" (*Editorial Comments on the Life and Work of Mary Baker Eddy,* p. 42).

Regarding the purpose and spirit of this book, I quote from the same source this deep appreciation (*ibid.*, p. 43): "In the assurance she has brought to doubt, the hope with which she has routed despair, the strength that has been given to weakness, the courage that has supplanted cowardice, the health that has banished wretchedness, the glory of the everlasting day into which she has marshaled the wanderers in night's terror—thus, in the grandeur and the permanence and the mercy of her works, she stands justified."

The other writings of Mary Baker Eddy, which she describes as "indispensable to the . . . student," seem to me to be the records of her own demonstration of *Science and Health*. They are the breaking of the bread of Life contained in the textbook, and are inspired by the same divine Spirit.

Her conviction of the spiritual origin of the By-Laws in our *Church Manual* is shown in these words in *Miscellaneous Writings* (p. 148): "They were impelled by a power not one's own."

In regard to our Lesson-Sermon, which is carrying the inspired Word over the entire world, no one doubts the divine appointment of its message. Mrs. Eddy once told us how this appointment came about. "My students were preaching," she said, "and were sending me copies of their sermons. They grew worse and worse. Finally one came which was so great a mixture that if I had not known the fact, I should not have been able to tell whether the writer were a Christian Scientist, a spiritualist or a theosophist. I said to myself, 'Something must be done and at once.' I withdrew from all other work, and in solitude and almost ceaseless prayer I sought and found God's will. At the end of three weeks I received the answer, and it came to me as naturally as dawns the morning light. 'Why, of course, the Bible and *Science and Health*.' " And now every week it is read to us from the *Christian Science Quarterly* that these sermons are "divinely authorized." That our Leader regarded also *The Christian Science Journal* and other publications as founded by the same divine Spirit, is evidenced in an incident which occurred in 1896. A number of letters from Christian Scientists, and addressed to Mrs. Eddy, were published in the *Journal*. Of this she writes (*Miscellaneous Writings*, p. 155), "If my own students cannot spare time to write to God,—when they address me I shall be apt to forward their letters to Him as our common Parent, and by way of *The Christian Science Journal.*"

As to the origin of *The Christian Science Monitor,* we may glance at past history. It is known that Mrs. Eddy had long in mind the publishing of a daily newspaper, and that she was waiting upon God to direct her. In 1907 there was launched against her what is known as the "Next Friends" suit. A leading daily in this country assumed a hostile attitude toward Christian Science and, in company with other enemies of our Cause, entered a suit against her, preferring malicious charges. Neither Mrs. Eddy's years, her womanhood, nor her blameless life deterred these ruthless enemies. It was especially hoped to hale Mrs. Eddy into court, where she could be ill-treated. The proceedings dragged through most of that year. All the charges were completely disproved and the case dismissed. How did the Leader herself look at this extraordinary proceeding? In spite of the malice directed toward her, and the reflection upon her lifework, she passed through this fiery trial, and began at once to plan good in return. And so *The Christian Science Monitor* was born. Like Christianity, it began in the manger of humility, but it was attended by the song of angels, and gifts from the simple-hearted and the wise.

In enumerating the writings of our great Leader, it must not be forgotten that she is the author of that profound work, *Christ and Christmas,* and of hymns and poems unspeakably dear to those who study them, which have carried physical healing and spiritual comfort to unnumbered sorrowing ones the world over. The rhythm of Spirit breathes its tender cadence of love through them all, recalling her own words that "Beauty is a thing of life, which dwells forever in the eternal Mind" (*Science and Health,* p. 247).

While every Christian Scientist has the privilege of distributing these sacred writings, the opportunity of doing so in the appointed order belongs especially to our Reading Rooms and our

Distribution Committees. Mrs. Eddy once spoke of "home" as "your calm, sacred retreat." We may think of our Reading Rooms, too, as a spiritual home and sacred retreat for the church members, as well as for inquirers. In them is spread a banquet of sustaining food for the seeker after healing of mind and body; the doubting, the distressed, the bewildered, the weary, may find in the shelter of the Reading Room the quiet and peace in which to ponder and pray, and to gain direction from the intimate Love which is ever seeking to find that which is lost, to heal that which is broken, and to comfort "as one whom his mother comforteth." Our Leader has provided in the *Manual* that no reading be done in a Reading Room except that of her writings, the Bible, and our authorized publications, and that secular matters be not discussed, that this atmosphere of calm and holy meditation may be always found there. May our church members realize more fully the purpose of the Reading Rooms, and avail themselves more often of the tender care shown in providing them.

Our Leader has made it clear throughout her writings that the purpose of these writings is to enrich our lives by restoring the lost element of spiritual healing. Jesus said, "I am come that they might have life, and that they might have it more abundantly," and St. John has added that the written word was given that we might believe, and that, believing, we might have life (John 20:31). Christian Science is the flowering of that believing—believing expanding into spiritual understanding, which the written word has brought us. Let us hold in our forever consciousness that Christian Science is the Comforter promised by the Founder of Christianity, and that it is the complete and final revelation of absolute Principle. It comes to give us "beauty for ashes, the oil of joy for mourning, the garment of praise for the spirit of heaviness" (Isaiah 61:3); to show us the way to live and to live "more abundantly," that we might be called "trees of righteousness, the planting of the Lord, that he might be glorified."

As a parting word, I wish to read a paragraph from a letter written by our loved Leader, which reveals the spiritual animus and purpose of her writings, and of her whole lifework. It was sent to one Christian Scientist, but is a benediction falling tenderly upon the heart of every one of us: "The Love that looks on this hour must be filling your heart with its Divine Presence, and will hear all your pure prayers to be perfect, and Mother's prayer to keep my child under the shelter of His wings."

An Intimate Picture of Our Leader's Final Class

SUE HARPER MIMS

O n opening the annual association meeting of her pupils held after her return from Concord, New Hampshire, Mrs. Mims read the tenth chapter of Luke, which she told us was read by the First Reader, Mr. Ezra M. Buswell, in the morning service at First Church of Christ, Scientist, in Concord. She stated that each one there felt that he had been told to read that chapter, and that the number of the class to be examined by Mrs. Eddy was indicated in the verse, "The Lord appointed other seventy also." This proved to be the case, as the number called by Mary Baker Eddy was seventy, although owing to the short notice of the call three were unable to be present.

Mrs. Mims then spoke informally, and substantially as follows:

I am just going to begin at the very beginning, and tell you everything I can possibly recall of my visit to Concord. On last Wednesday I received a letter from Mrs. Eddy, requesting me to meet her at four o'clock on the following Sunday afternoon at the Christian Science Hall in Concord. The letter stated "strictly confidential," so that no one knew where I was going but my husband, who got my ticket for me.

I was in Chattanooga Thursday night, but on Friday morning I left for Boston, arriving there at nine o'clock Saturday night. I immediately looked up the Sunday trains for Concord, and found there was but one, which left at one o'clock. I was too impatient to wait until that time; I really think I could not have slept if I had had to wait until the next day, but I found that there was a paper train which left Boston at two o'clock in the morning.

I reached Concord at five, and went right to the hotel. I did not feel at all uncomfortable about being out on the street alone at that very early hour, and did not feel tired. I rested at the hotel until time for church. The service was beautiful. As I have told you, Mr. Buswell read this beautiful chapter from Luke. I met very many that you would all know. Mr. and Mrs. Kimball [Mr. Edward A. Kimball of Chicago] were there, and Judge and Mrs. Hanna [Judge Septimus J. Hanna, one-time Editor of *The Christian Science Journal*]. There were many delightful people there, and the hotels were full.

All Concord is realizing the material good that Mrs. Eddy's residence there is bringing to the town. It has brought them much patronage in every way. They are waking up somewhat to see the spiritual gain, but they are realizing very forcibly the material benefit that Christian Science is to their beautiful little town—for it is a very beautiful little place. It is an educational point and is both active and interesting.

At four o'clock, or rather about three-thirty, everyone was seated in the little hall where First Church of Christ, Scientist, holds its meetings. On the first bench Mrs. Eddy placed those who had demonstrated a great deal from the simple study of the textbook, *Science and Health with Key to the Scriptures*. One member of the class had been healed of almost every kind of disease known to mortal mind—consumption, heart trouble, tumor, some hereditary claims—everything. She was exceedingly interesting. She was healed by reading St. John, and she had, a short time afterward, a vision of being led to the light of Truth.

There were a number of others who had had similar experiences, and our dear teacher seemed to have a peculiarly tender feeling for them. Another was a prominent lawyer and a most interesting man. When Mrs. Eddy first heard from him, she immediately wrote him not to study with anyone else but to come to her—she felt something so wonderfully receptive in his thought.

Back of that bench were those who were students of her students, and back of them were those who were her students and who were going through this class which she called a Normal class. It was, however, principally an examination with some teaching.

I would like to say something about the personnel of the class, which was very remarkable. There were lawyers, physicians, judges, businessmen and, what was to me the most beautiful of all, several young men of under thirty years of age, who had given up every kind of business occupation just to become Christian Scientists. There were also some very lovely young women. A physician was there, a splendid man who abandoned his profession upon coming into Christian Science, and a woman who was for twelve years the physician at Wellesley College and who gave up this work to follow Truth. Another prominent physician was also present with his wife, and many others. You would not often see a group of such refined, distinguished people collected together anywhere else in this country. All were noble and highly intellectual. But the sweetest thing to me was to see those young men—just leaving all for Christ.

One of them was in the boardinghouse where a young woman and I went, as we were to stay over for the Wednesday evening meeting. I remember we passed his door, which was standing open, and as I saw his Bible and *Science and Health* lying open there, it gave me such a feeling of love and tenderness to think of these young, pure thoughts going out into the world and radiating this truth.

So you can see that the personnel of the class was really extraordinary. I forgot to say that there were also two editors—young, intellectual, manly. One member of the class came from London, and another from Scotland, so that the range from Maine to California, from England and Scotland, was really marvelous.

Presently Mrs. Eddy appeared, promptly on the minute, for she is a "minute woman." Everything in her house moves in accord with Principle. I do not suppose there is a businessman in the world more methodical or more absolutely accurate than

Mrs. Eddy. She said that Christian Scientists should be the most methodical people on earth because they recognize one fixed Principle. So it was promptly at four o'clock that she came into the room, and I am going to tell you just how she looked and how she was dressed. She walks very quickly and smoothly. She is the most graceful of women. Around her neck was a little black and white ermine cape. Her beautiful white hair was in loose waves or curls around her brow. She sat in a big red-cushioned chair, which made a beautiful background for her, and when she threw back her cape it revealed a very handsome black silk dress. The skirt was of black moiré, and the waist was of white silk covered with net and heavily trimmed with jet. She wore a diamond cross given her by one of her students, and an exquisite pin presented to her by the Daughters of the American Revolution. She wore white kid gloves.

She is the very picture of refined elegance, and were I to try to describe her to you exactly, the difficulty would be to find words to express how fine she is, how delicate, how sensitive, how exquisite. The fineness of her nature shows in her very appearance, and yet with all this refinement and elegance you have never seen any human being look so meek and so holy. All of this appearance of richness one really loses sight of, as he sees this wonderful meekness and sweetness, and I think everyone who looked at her as she sat there found his eyes grow moist with love and tenderness for her.

One would be apt to think that a woman who would telegraph to every part of our country—perhaps to a judge, a lawyer, a doctor—to come and spend a few hours with her, saying that it would be a blessing to him, would be an aggressive person, a woman who felt her power and enjoyed ordering others around. Indeed, mortal mind seems to get the idea sometimes that she is stern and arbitrary. "Oh, yes," they say, "she rules them with a rod of iron; they do just what she tells them to." But if they could only see her, they would know that her motive is simply her divine love for them and for the Cause. She is obliged to know what she is; she must know that it means a blessing to come within the direct radiation of her love—but you have never in all your life seen anyone so gentle and courteous and humble and meek. You have never seen so little human will, for she knows that human will is the devil, and all that she does is done by reflecting divine Love. And you feel this; you feel as tender as you would to a little child, and at the same time you realize the wonderful grasp and comprehensiveness of her mind. As you see more of her, you see the most delicate play of wit, and in a gentle, sweet way, the most delicate sarcasm.

She sat there and spoke to us in the most graceful way. If she tells you to do anything, she asks you to do it, in the sweetest, most pleading way you ever saw. She said how glad she was to see us all, how she had heard of us as teachers, lecturers, and workers in the Field, and had heard of our work with great satisfaction.

Then she began by doing just as we do in our class, asking each one, "What is God to you?" She pointed out that the most important thing in the world is to know God, and to know what God is. It was beautiful to watch her face as they answered. You have never seen so strange a face. She reminds me of that paragraph in *Science and Health* (p. 213), "Mortal mind is the harp of many strings, discoursing either discord or harmony according as the hand, which sweeps over it, is human or divine." When the replies were scientific and clear, her face was something beyond words to express. There came into it the look of one who lives in the realm of Soul. As they grasped the absolute truth, her eyes seemed to look into the realm of Spirit, and it is something one cannot describe.

One of the young men when asked this question, "What is God to you?" said, "God is Love, God is Life, Truth, Spirit. He is All-in-all; He is destruction." You should have seen her face; but she let him go on, listening to him in perfect courtesy. He was one of the young men whom she loved very dearly, and when he had finished she said gently, as I recollect it:

"Now, John, you have said that God is Life, Truth, Love,

Spirit, All-in-all, and you have said that He is destruction. Will you tell me how God is destruction? Is there anything but God? What is there then to destroy?"

He answered quickly, and humbly: "Nothing, Mother, God is All, and there is nothing else. He only destroys what seems to be unlike Himself." But the changing expression of her face during this incident impressed me very much. One could really see in her face whether error or truth was being voiced—so delicate is it, so sensitive—and it made me realize what she must have suffered when she first saw what the truth is, and then found that she must go down into the depths of error; how she cried, "Oh, let me not into the secret." She did not want to investigate the secrets of error. (See *Miscellaneous Writings*, pp. 222–223.)

When she had been around the class, and everyone had answered, she said, as I remember: "You have told me wonderful things today. Now you must live up to them; you must prove them. That is what Christian Science is—it is practical. God is your Life, and there is no evil."

Then she told us something of her experience when she first saw the truth. She said the first revelation that came to her was that she could not die. She saw Life, and that it was impossible for her to die. And then she told us that three times she had raised the dead. I could not help thinking of Jesus, first raising the little maid, then the young man, and then Lazarus. She told us of one instance; she did not tell us of the others.

I think it was a long time ago. She said that she was sent for, and when she came the mother of the child was crying, "Oh, she is dead; she is dead." She put the mother out of the room, and went in and took the child in her arms. In an hour she called the mother, and the child was running across the floor to meet her.

Once she spoke substantially as follows:

"We are all learning together, and I must tell you of some of the funny things I used to do when I first saw that I had this wonderful power." (I think that her work has always been exceedingly quick.)

"My family and the friends around me saw what was done and knew that if they sent for me they would be well, but I could not make them acknowledge it. I could not make them admit what had done the healing work. One day I said, 'Oh, I *must* make them acknowledge it; I must make them see that God does this.' Sometimes as soon as they sent for me they would be healed, before I could get there, and then they would not *know* that it was God who had done it. So one day when I was called to see a child, I was so anxious to have the power of Truth acknowledged that I said to myself, 'He *must* not get well until I get there.' Of course that was not right, for I knew I must leave it all to God, but pride had come in and I had lost my humility, and the patient was not healed. Then I saw my rebuke, and when I reached home I threw myself on the floor, put my head in my hands, and prayed that I might not be for one moment touched with the thought that I was anything or did anything; I realized that this was God's work and I reflected Him. Then the child was healed." This was the way she learned her lesson.

Then after she had finished speaking, her students arose and gave their experiences. Judge Hanna said that he had once been the instrument through which death had been destroyed. I do not think he said that the patient had really passed on but that it was the very last moment. He said that he went into the room, and had such a realization of Life that the work was instantly done.

The young man, of whom I have previously spoken, arose to speak but was so overcome with emotion that he had to sit down. It was quite a few moments before he could proceed. He said that Christian Science had come to him in a marvelous burst of light. Three times he had a vision of wonderful, intense light, in which he was simply bathed, a light beyond the brightness of the sun or any light that is known. I have never seen anything like her face when he told of it. It simply quivered. Her look was wonderful as she said, as I recall it: "Yes, I felt it when you wrote to me, and you are nearer to me in the resurrection thought than anyone I ever touched. That is the reason I told you not to go to anyone else to be taught, but to come to me."

There were a number of other interesting experiences. One lady said that once or twice a brilliant light had flooded her book as she was reading.

Mrs. Eddy, when the class was over, said she had not known before how many days she would teach, but this class had been so satisfactory that she would have only one more session, which would be the next day. She said she would make no charge for this class. "When first establishing this Cause," I recall her saying, "I needed money, but I have now learned that God is with me, that He gives me everything, and I cannot lack." A little later she added, as I recollect, "When you stand before a mirror and look at your reflection, it is the same as the original. Now you are God's reflection. If His hands are full, your hands are full, if you image Him. You cannot know lack. I have learned now that He does give us everything."

Then she asked us questions. One was, "What is the best way to do instantaneous healing?" Many arose. Some said, "Realize the ever-presence of good"; others, "Deny the claims of evil." There were many answers, but when they had finished, she said, as I remember: "I will tell you the way to do it. It is to love! Just live love—be it—love, love, love. Do not know anything but Love. Be all love. There is nothing else. That will do the work. It will heal everything; it will raise the dead. *Be* nothing but love."

Then there came up what was, to me, the most interesting question in the whole class. Someone said, "But, Mother, are we not to discriminate between good and evil?" She answered substantially as follows: "Ah, now you have asked me what is to me the hardest thing in Christian Science! Yes, you must see and denounce evil. The Bible tells us that Jesus was God's chosen because he loved righteousness, but the Bible does not stop there. It says, 'and hated iniquity'! So often have I longed to see and know only Love—only the good—but I have not dared. I *must* uncover and rebuke and *hate* iniquity."

134

This was very valuable to us all. To her this is the greatest struggle of all, the hardest thing in Science, but when one *loves* righteousness, one *hates* iniquity.

Then she spoke of the absurdity of the literal translation of the Bible. Everything in the Bible, she told us, has its spiritual interpretation, though many see only the literal meaning. And she added the following humorous story: "Once there was a man who engaged another man to hoe in his field for him. In the middle of the day the workman came to the employer and said, 'I want to go and get some water for I am thirsty.' 'No, you cannot go,' said the employer. 'Why when I have been working hard and am thirsty,' said the man, 'can I not go and get some water?' 'Because it is contrary to the Bible,' was the reply. 'How is that?' asked the other. 'Why, the Bible says, "Ho, every one that thirsteth"!' "

Once in the course of the examination she said substantially:

"My dear ones, I would love it very much—I would feel it a great favor—if you would translate for me into the new tongue some passages from the Bible. Who will do this for me?" Her tone was so gentle and soft and pleading. A splendid, stalwart boy arose and, as no one else seemed to, I stood up. Then someone said: "Mother, we will all do it; we all want to do it." So she found the twenty-fourth chapter of Luke (you can see how she dwells in the resurrection thought) and asked the young man to translate the first verse spiritually for her. It was, "Now upon the first day of the week, very early in the morning, they came unto the sepulchre, bringing the spices which they had prepared, and certain others with them."

He began to explain it, stumbling along like a big schoolboy: "Well, Mother, you know they were women, and women have the highest idea of God." Here, as I remember, she said softly, "I don't know about that." "They saw a new idea of God," he continued, "and they brought spices, which were their loving thoughts."

When he had finished, she called me and made me come and

sit upon the platform by her side, saying she wanted them all to see me. Then she asked me to translate the second verse. I did not remember it, but when she handed me the Bible I found it was, "And they found the stone rolled away from the sepulchre."

"The stone," I said, "was the concentrated human belief that life was limited, and they saw that Life had rolled it away and that man was immortal—that he was never born and never dies." I closed by saying, "They saw what our beloved mother has through *Science and Health* enabled us to see. Through the book we have seen all that they saw and more, and we owe it all to her, to this beloved one who is God's messenger today."

When I had given her back the book and gone to my seat, she said in effect:

"You have given a very beautiful exegesis of the text, but I have one objection—I may say I have one fault to find—it was not necessary to mention me."

Then I wish you could have seen that class. One arose with wet eyes and said, "Mother, how could we forget you?" Judge Hanna got up, and it was one of the most heart-rending things I ever heard in my life, as he said:

"Mother, let me tell you this. Sometimes all the machinations of evil that are conceivable to the human mind seem to be hurled at us, and sometimes for days the world seems black. Every argument that the ingenuity of evil can suggest whispers, trying to hide your mission, and the light returns only when we see you as you are—the revelator of this Truth."

Others spoke on the same line. It was the most beautiful thing, and you see that had to be brought out. She had to be acknowledged, and yet while they were speaking you have never seen such humility, such self-effacement, in your life. And then she said, according to my recollection: "My dear children, if you had not seen it, I should have had to teach you this. I could not have avoided telling you that when my students become blinded to me as the one through whom Truth has come in this age, they miss the path. I would have had to tell you."

The tears of joy were on her face, and that strange, wonderful look that perhaps no mortal face ever had, since Jesus and Paul. Perhaps no face was ever more tender. It was filled with meekness and humility, yet the responsibility was hers of making us know that when we do not see her as she is, we lose the way.

There is not a day of my life that I do not declare at least once, often twice, that malicious animal magnetism cannot blind me to her. We must fix our gaze on Principle, think of God, and yet we must recognize who she is.

At the close of the class she said in effect, "I cannot tell you the joy this class is to me. I am so pleased and satisfied. I feel the years roll off me!" What a wonderful thing to say!

There are no words to tell what the radiation of love, just from her presence, is. She gave us a beautiful interpretation of what it means to "run, and not be weary; . . . walk, and not faint" (Isaiah 40:31). She takes it right into metaphysics. When we are working to overcome error, or are handling a case that does not seem to yield, we shall not be discouraged or wearied by the work, nor can there be any reaction. We shall go on without suffering or being weary, even though the demonstration is slow.

She told us one thing that we should all remember. She said, as I recall, "Now I want you to speak distinctly. When you speak distinctly it shows your mental quality. Speak as if you had something that you wanted the world to hear. Speak loud and strong and distinctly." Her own voice is very clear.

Of our source of supply she said in substance, "It is like a scale. On one side is the infinite good—that is the side of Spirit. Everything we put in the scale of Spirit is in the scale of infinity, but materiality means limitation, and everything we put in the side of matter, we put in the scale of limitation.

"In the human," I recall her adding, "it is good for us to think of God as our Father and Mother, with us every moment, giving us everything, clothing us, feeding us, giving us everything good and beautiful, caring for our human bodies. But in metaphysics man is the image of God. Man never was a child to grow. In metaphysics, man reflects all that God is. God is the trinity, Life, Truth, and Love; man is the idea of Life, Truth, and Love. Man is just as old as God, and he reflects all that God is and all that God has. We must live in the thought of His ever-present infinite Life and Love."

Of making her gifts, she said in effect: "I want no material gifts. I want spiritual gifts. I would rather have one outstanding healing than all the gifts on earth. These are the gifts I want—your own spiritual growth, your own demonstrations."

I think now that I have told you all. What I wanted to make you see was her wonderful meekness, humility, gentleness, courtesy, and love. I do not think anyone in this room will ever adore the personality of Mrs. Eddy, but you will love her and reverence her as the highest manifestation of Love that is in the world, or that has been for eighteen hundred years, as the Leader of the greatest movement that ever was, the movement that is establishing the kingdom of God on earth; as the one through whom God is being enthroned in the hearts of humanity. I was so glad that I could say what God is, in the exact words of the book.

I did not have a private talk with Mrs. Eddy. At the close of the class she shook hands with us all.

Mrs. Eddy and the Class of 1898

EMMA C. SHIPMAN

Tonight, in thought, will you turn back time, and go to a modest little hall in Concord, New Hampshire, recently provided by Rev. Mary Baker Eddy for Christian Science services.

It is Sunday morning, November 20, 1898. An unusually large number are in the hall for the morning service. About seventy have come from various parts of the world. The First Reader has chosen his Scripture reading from the tenth chapter of Luke, beginning: "The Lord appointed other seventy also . . . . Therefore said he unto them, The harvest truly is great, but the labourers are few: pray ye therefore the Lord of the harvest, that he would send forth labourers into his harvest."

How these words burn in the hearts of many present, for they know that soon they will be commissioned to go forth to labor for the Cause of Christian Science! Doubtless they are praying that they may be worthy of that commission.

After the morning service they return to their hotels or homes, for some reside in Concord, to wait until four o'clock, when they are to meet their teacher, Mrs. Eddy, and have their first lesson.

Promptly, at the appointed hour, those whom our Leader had chosen are in their places. Mr. Edward A. Kimball is on the platform to read a letter from Mrs. Eddy, from which I shall quote: *"Beloved Christian Scientists:—*

"Your prompt presence in Concord at my unexplained call witnesses your fidelity to Christian Science and your spiritual unity with your Leader. . . . This opportunity is designed to impart a fresh impulse to our spiritual attainments, the great need of which I daily discern. I have awaited the right hour, and to be called of God to contribute my part towards this result. . . . What

I have to say may not require more than one lesson. This, however, must depend on results. But the lessons will certainly not exceed three in number. . . ." (*The First Church of Christ, Scientist, and Miscellany,* 243:20-1, 244:10, 24–26.)

After the letter is read, Mrs. Eddy, dignified, beautiful, poised, comes to the platform. The class rises instantly, reverently and silently to greet her. With a cordial smile and a motion of her hand, she bids us be seated. The spirituality which our teacher expresses is so penetrating, so enlightening, that apparently without effort she turns us from her personality to her message.

She reminds us that some in the class she has not met, so she will call their names and ask them to rise, one by one. As we do so, her clear glance seems to read us, and at the same time to reassure us.

Now the lessons begin. Our first subject is God. His nearness and goodness are brought to our attention, until one feels the unspeakable depth of the riches, both of the wisdom and love of God.

Our teacher calls on some of the members of the class to tell what term for God means the most to them. The majority say it is Love. A young woman who has recently lost her mother, says that Father-Mother God means the most to her. Mrs. Eddy's tender, compassionate look as this answer is given, shows that she knows this pupil's need, and the entire class feels the comforting sympathy in her voice as she gives her approval of the answer.

One of the judges in the class declares that Principle means the most to him. We can see, from the merry twinkle in Mrs. Eddy's eye, as she gives her approving recognition of his answer, that her look is almost saying, "That is just what I expected from you."

Two in the class have answered questions in tones that are inaudible. Our teacher says, as I recall: Speak up! When you speak so you cannot be heard, you virtually say, "I have nothing worthy of saying."

In trying to tell of our Leader's instruction, one feels the inadequacy of words to describe a spiritual experience.

When she said, after showing us the need of knowing God more intimately, "Your God is your life," we felt, Here is the work of eternity. Here is our starting point—to begin to know God.

Mrs. Eddy was perfectly natural, she was ever alert, with a keen sense of wit and humor, and at the same time, her listening attitude to hear what God would give her to say, was apparent.

One felt the great breadth of her nature which enabled her, in such rich amplitude, to meet all the varying needs of her large class.

Mrs. Eddy presented two aspects to her pupils which were so perfectly blended that one gained, in her presence, the feeling of her perfect harmony with Life.

One aspect was her clear and unfailing spiritual sense; her unswerving reliance on God; her consciousness of His ever-presence, and of His nearness, as a friend is near.

The other aspect was her great humanity; her uncommon, common sense, as shown in her practical application of Jesus' teachings to all the little things of everyday living.

This perfect blending of the spiritual and practical gave us an example of what makes a real Christian Scientist. Who but Mrs. Eddy could have written of Jesus, "Through the magnitude of his human life, he demonstrated the divine Life" (*Science and Health,* p. 54).

She spoke to us with deepest reverence and understanding of Christ Jesus, the Way-shower, and pointed out the vital necessity of following him.

She called to our attention, as she had to earlier classes, the experience of the three disciples on the mount of transfiguration. She quoted Peter's words, "Master, it is good for us to be here: and let us make three tabernacles; one for thee, and one for Moses, and one for Elias" (Mark 9:5). Our teacher said, in substance, that these three tabernacles are to be in our hearts. One for Christ Jesus, to be built by self-consecration on the foundation of victory over sin, sickness, and death. One for Moses, or the law, built by our strict adherence to the Ten Commandments. The third, for Elias, was for prophetic vision, which can be built only as we are motivated by all that is high and holy.

As she talked, her spiritual insight, her oneness with the Father, gave a radiance and richer meaning to statements in her writings already familiar to us.

At times, she illustrated a point in metaphysics with an anecdote or short story. Once, when she had made us all laugh heartily, she said, as I recall: I like to have my students laugh. A good laugh often breaks mesmerism.

She made it clear that one must overcome the instincts of the carnal mind—go down on one's knees, as it were—and struggle with error until the battle with sense and self is fought and the victory won.

Her method in teaching was first to question the pupils. Her clear insight could detect at once whether they answered by merely repeating the words or from an understanding heart. After listening to the answers, she unfolded spiritual truths according to the need.

She told us that the home of the Christian Scientist is in the understanding of God, his affections and interests are there, and his abiding place is there.

When she asked the members of the class for a definition of the Trinity, it was evident that the answers were not perfect. Mrs. Eddy then made a brief explanation, and a few weeks later she sent each member the following:

THE TRINITY

Father, is man's divine Principle, Love.
Son, is God's man—His image, or spiritual idea.
Holy Ghost, is Divine Science, the Messiah or Comforter.
Jesus in the flesh was the prophet or wayshower to Life,
    Truth, Love, and out of the flesh Jesus was the Christ,
    the spiritual idea or image and likeness of God.

MARY BAKER EDDY

This was but one instance of her loving care for her pupils.

When she was explaining the necessity of reducing evil, to use her words, "to its proper denominator,—nobody and nothing" (*Miscellaneous Writings*, p. 108), she put her hands before her, on a level with each other, as if weighing something in each, and she said so earnestly, as I recall her words, Always balance evil in the scale with nothingness. One saw clearly that evil and nothing exactly balance.

Our teacher called for questions from the class, and answered each one with the ease, grace, and certainty of one who had first solved for herself the problems of human experience.

After she had talked about the great need of love in everything we do, a pupil asked, "Do you mean love of person?" Mrs. Eddy replied, in substance, No, I mean love of good. Then she was asked, "How shall we know whether our love is personal or impersonal?" Her reply, in substance, was, When your love requires an object to call it forth, you will know it is personal; when it flows out freely to all, you will know it is impersonal.

A pupil asked: "Why is it that our healing work is not always the same? One day, our cases are healed, and another day, with the same amount of work, a case is not healed." Mrs. Eddy had a pencil in her hand; she balanced it on one finger, and then, tipping it to one side, she said, as I recall, It is because we have too much weight on the side of matter; then, tipping the pencil in the opposite direction, she added that some day we shall have more weight on the side of Spirit; then we shall always heal the sick.

When the lessons were finished, we were fully convinced that Mrs. Eddy had broken the bread of Life with us; that she had given us more in those two lessons than any other teacher on earth could give in any number of lessons.

A member of the class, Judge Septimus J. Hanna, then Editor of the Christian Science periodicals, wrote in *The Christian Science Journal,* of December 1898, as follows: "Only two lessons! but such lessons! It were futile to attempt a description or review.

Only those who have sat under this wondrous teaching can form a conjecture of what these classes were. The Decalogue and Sermon on the Mount were brought before the class, not in epitome, but in marvelous elaboration. The whole Bible, in verity, was held up in vivid review, and its mighty, yet simple and practical, spiritual import, illustrated in language of superb clearness and picturesque beauty,—faultless in symmetry, majestic in the depth of its spiritual significance. To say that this teaching lifted one Heavenward—Godward,—that it sank deep into the consciousness of all present, is only feebly to hint at the actual fact."

The question is often asked, "Why did some in the class receive a C.S.D. degree, while the majority received a C.S.B. degree, and all had a Normal course certificate?" The answer is simple. According to the rules of her College, Mrs. Eddy— with one or two exceptions—gave the C.S.D. degree only to those who had had at least two courses under her instruction. Only about one fourth of the class had previously had her teaching. When Mrs. Eddy was asked why she chose so many young people for the class, she replied, in substance, Because I want my teaching carried on.

Our teacher followed her direction to teachers in *Science and Health*. I quote, "Do not dismiss students at the close of a class term, feeling that you have no more to do for them" (p. 454). She answered our letters or had her secretary do so. She called us to her home at different times and did all in her power to promote our progress.

Our beloved teacher gave enlightenment to her pupils but not dictation. After she had made clear the Principle and rules of Christian Science and had illustrated their practical value, she left her pupils free to work out their individual problems, guided by our textbook, *Science and Health*.

May we all carry steadily the torch which Mary Baker Eddy, the

Discoverer and Founder of Christian Science, our beloved Leader and teacher, has lighted for us. May it glow ever brighter and brighter, through the generations to come, unto that perfect day when they shall all know God, from the least of them unto the greatest.

An Interview with Mary Baker Eddy, and Other Memories

MARY STEWART

*I*t should be understood that, when I quote Mrs. Eddy in the address which I am about to give, the wording is as I vividly recall it, and is substantially correct.

I wish that you all, especially those of you who never saw our Leader, Mary Baker Eddy, or heard her speak, might have been with me one day in January 1901, as I waited a few moments for her in her library at Pleasant View, and felt, before seeing her, the loving presence I was invited to enter. She came with a light step and a pleasant greeting. I saw again this beautiful, gentle woman—daintily gowned, ready to go for her usual drive after my call. Her hair was silvery white, soft, and becomingly dressed; her face unwrinkled and lovely in coloring; her expression vivacious and constantly changing with her thoughts; her eyes large, deep and blue, sometimes laughing, sometimes tender, sometimes sad for a moment as she spoke of a lawsuit, to which she was having to give much time, and of some conditions in the Field. Her voice was colorful, firm, refined, and she talked with her lips, her eyes, her hands, and from her heart.

Our Leader exemplified her words in *Christian Science Series* (Vol. I, No. 1). There she speaks of the effect of accumulative years and says, "The added wisdom of age and experience is strength, not weakness, and we should understand this, expect it, and know that it is so, then it would appear."

I was in Concord in response to a telegram to come at once. I found five other Scientists at Christian Science Hall, and learned that we were called to do some preliminary work toward winning a suit which had been brought against Mrs. Eddy and some of the officers of The Mother Church. Living at a greater distance than the others, I arrived a day later. They had had an interview with our Leader that afternoon, but in the evening, with her unfailing graciousness, she sent one of her secretaries with a message to me and an invitation to call on her the next day. The message she sent was this: "Tell her that her prompt obedience to the call will ensure to her life, health, and heaven." This interview seemed to me a foretaste of heaven.

When Mrs. Eddy entered the room that day, she seated herself in a chair close to mine and at once asked, "What did So-and-so [the secretary] say to you last evening?" I replied, "Mother, he said that he had discovered self-justification in himself." With the merriest laugh she said, "Oh, he did not discover it, I did!" Then followed the most precious three quarters of an hour I have ever experienced except in her class.

She talked earnestly of the welfare of the Cause and of the Field; of how error tried to separate some of her oldest students from the church; of her last class and of teaching in general; and of some of her early healings.

She told of a healing of heart disease, and of cancer, instantaneously, and emphasized the necessity for giving much time and consecration to the work of healing, adding, "I cannot help healing." It was her great love and spirituality which made healing as natural to her as it was to Jesus. In class she had taught us that it is "Love" that heals the dying.

Continuing to talk about Christian Science healing she said: "The worst evil is to go to a bed of sickness and say: God is All. God is Love. You are not sick." She spoke with scorn of such statements made coldly and superficially, and indicated that that sort of practice sometimes amounted to neglect of a case and brought criticism from physicians, saying: "If I were a physician I would have made the same criticisms, and they would have been just. How I decry such practice!" Then with a light in her eyes and filled with the power of Spirit she said, "Mother would say,

Arise and walk!" Like Jesus, our Leader healed quickly and permanently, not fearing to use the sword of the Spirit to separate evil from person.

Mrs. Eddy related some of the efforts of evil against her, saying that there were those who were working to separate churches, break up the ranks; "to separate from me," she said, "to break up my household." As she said this her face was illumined with the Christ-spirit—her look and attitude declaring her dominion. The threats of evil and their boastfulness seemed so absurd, impossible, and impudent that I laughed. Instantly she said: "If you take it that way, perhaps you could stand. Yes, you can—and having done all, stand." This recalls her statement in *Unity of Good* (p. 17), "A lie has only one chance of successful deception,—to be accounted true."

As we stood together a moment before she went for her drive, she remarked, "I feel that I have known you always." That exactly expressed what I had been feeling—so gracious was she in her ability to make one feel at home. We had all felt this unity with her in class.

During the time the group of Scientists were working together it was evident that Mrs. Eddy was constantly listening for God's direction. She sent us instructions about how to work, then told us to wait; then again came definite instruction. Ever did she exemplify her words in *Miscellaneous Writings* (Pref., p. xii), "With armor on, I continue the march, command and countermand." When that part of the work for which this group had been called was accomplished, she directed us to return to our homes. She wrote: "I deeply thank you for your Christlikeness in coming and going at the word. Our Master did just this. I have done it for thirty years."

Much of the spirit and letter of our Leader's last class have been given by other students in published articles, such as her statement of the Trinity; her teaching of God as Father, Mother, Shepherd, and other never-to-be-forgotten instruction. There was much to encourage and comfort the younger members of the class. She said: "I will lift you into the understanding." "All is God's; everything belongs to Him. You reflect it all." "I have made you learners."

She told us that in her early experience in Christian Science her work was so quick that people who sent for her were healed before she reached their homes, and often did not acknowledge that Christian Science had anything to do with their recovery.

In this class, through our teacher's pure love and spirituality, I caught an illuminating sense of *reflection*. Where there is reflection there is light. She handled animal magnetism from the standpoint of the allness of Spirit, reducing it to nothingness through the ever-present Christ-power.

Mrs. Eddy asked nothing for herself personally. As we understand her better, we can give more to the Cause for which she laid down all. Only as we recognize the revelator can we understand and obey the revelation. As the prophecies of Jesus and of John were fulfilled through her, so must we, her followers, do our part in fulfilling her prediction for the twentieth century (*Pulpit and Press,* p. 22): "Christ will give to Christianity his new name, and Christendom will be classified as Christian Scientists."

Some Precious Memories
of Mary Baker Eddy

CALVIN C. HILL
Compiled by Frances Thompson Hill

*M*y early religious training at home and in the Presbyterian church prepared me to accept and appreciate Christian Science when it was presented to me in an hour of great need. Two of my brothers and two sisters had passed on because of tuberculosis, and I was filled with fear that I too might be a victim, for I was manifesting symptoms of the disease. The following is part of my testimony which was published in the August 22, 1903, issue of the *Christian Science Sentinel:*

> In 1890 I gave up business in the East and went
> to try the high, dry climate of Colorado. I had been told
> that this was the only thing that would do me any per-
> manent good. During eight years prior to this time
> I had been taking medicine for several diseases with
> but temporary relief. In 1892, Christian Science was pre-
> sented to me by a fellow salesman who had been healed
> by reading *Science and Health*. For three years I refused to
> listen to any great extent to what was said to me by
> this friend as to what Christian Science could do for me.
> In 1895, however, having given the climate as well as
> new *materia medica* remedies almost five years' trial
> without any lasting benefit, I decided to give Christian
> Science a trial, and did so.

That which was causing me most distress when I turned to

Christian Science for healing was indigestion, for which medical treatment had been unavailing. I was healed of this malady in the first Christian Science treatment I received, and later all of my other infirmities and fears were dispelled by the light of Truth and Love as revealed in the Christian Science textbook, *Science and Health with Key to the Scriptures* by Mary Baker Eddy.

Naturally I wished to learn all I could about this wonderful spiritual truth which had so abundantly blessed me. I studied the textbook earnestly, and when the friend who had presented Christian Science to me said that he and his wife were moving to Boston in order to be at headquarters and render all possible service to the Cause of Christian Science, I decided to go to Boston at once where I could see Christian Science and Christian Scientists at work. This was early in 1895. Upon my arrival in Boston I obtained a position with an excellent firm dealing in carpets and draperies. Soon after this I met members of The Christian Science Board of Directors and other students of Mrs. Eddy.

The more I studied Mrs. Eddy's writings, together with the Bible, and the more I heard Christian Science discussed by its adherents and saw it exemplified in their daily lives, the more convinced I became that it was what Christ Jesus knew, taught, and proved in many wonderful works of healing. In spite of this, however, I was prejudiced against Mrs. Eddy, as will be seen in the following excerpt from my testimony:

> After coming to Boston, I began at once to attend The Mother Church services. At first I found much fault with the testimonies given at the weekly evening meetings, especially when Mrs. Eddy was referred to. My thought toward her had been poisoned by reading articles in the newspapers, magazines, etc., detrimental to her and to Christian Science. I was healed of this attitude of thought toward Mrs. Eddy, however, just as quickly and effectually as I was healed of dyspepsia, when one evening one of Mrs. Eddy's own students

arose in the meeting and said in part, "You can no more separate Mrs. Eddy from *Science and Health* than you can Moses from the Commandments, or Jesus from the Sermon on the Mount."

These statements healed me of my wrong thought toward Mrs. Eddy. With this healing I began to grow in the understanding of the teachings of Christian Science.

I have received great help from the *study* of the Bible and Mrs. Eddy's writings. "God is no respecter of persons." The promise is: "Seek, and ye shall find."

I am continually seeing in Mrs. Eddy's life the exemplification of her writings. Her life is proof to me that "one with God is a majority."

From the time of this awakening to a true estimate of Mrs. Eddy, I sought diligently to find her in her writings.

On Sunday, January 5, 1896, I had the inestimable privilege of being in The Mother Church when Mrs. Eddy came from her home at Pleasant View, Concord, New Hampshire, to give the Communion address. When the service had proceeded nearly to the point where the address was to be delivered, Mrs. Eddy entered the auditorium and walked down the aisle toward the rostrum. When she appeared the members of the congregation rose and remained standing until she was seated. After listening to the solo, Mrs. Eddy stepped forward, and in a voice resonant with spiritual power and beauty, and with articulation so distinct that not a syllable was lost, she gave the Communion address, which all may now read on pages 120–125 of *Miscellaneous Writings*.

A well-known feature writer, Miss Lilian Whiting, was present at this service, and her description of Mrs. Eddy was published in the *Chicago Inter-Ocean*. It read as follows:

> Mrs. Eddy is over seventy, yet her whole appearance is of a woman hardly more than half that age. She re-

tains her delicacy of complexion, with its transparent clearness and brilliant flush; her dark eyes are bright, her graceful figure might be that of a girl of twenty, and her whole bearing is full of energy and charm. Her hair is white, which is almost the only mark that time has made upon her. Her presence is one of great dignity, of beautiful repose, of infinite sweetness. . . .
A most remarkable figure in contemporary life is Mary Baker Eddy.

My first meeting with Mrs. Eddy came about in connection with the firm where I was employed, John H. Pray and Sons Company of Boston. On a Saturday in April 1899, Mrs. Laura Sargent, a member of Mrs. Eddy's household, and James A. Neal, already a well-known worker in Christian Science, came to the store to select samples of floor coverings for Pleasant View, Mrs. Eddy's home in Concord, New Hampshire. After they had made their selections and had departed, I found that we lacked sufficient yardage of some of the material. Also I believed that something more suitable for Mrs. Eddy's home could be obtained. The following day I went to New York, and early on Monday morning I made further selections of carpeting which seemed to me more appropriate. On Tuesday morning I took these samples to Concord.

I well remember that bright, spring morning. On arriving at Pleasant View, Mrs. Sargent received me and showed me to the back parlor, where I arranged the samples. I had barely time to glance around at the general color scheme and furnishings when the members of the household began to gather. While we were chatting pleasantly Mrs. Eddy entered the room.

I am often asked how I felt on meeting Mrs. Eddy for the first time. I can truthfully say that I felt no strangeness. People are what their thoughts are, and I already knew many of Mrs. Eddy's thoughts. I had become acquainted with them through her writings.

Characteristically, I did not notice what Mrs. Eddy was wearing. I was aware of her erect carriage and dignity but much more aware of a sweet motherliness. I thought of my own mother, the noblest character I had hitherto known.

As I rose and took her outstretched hand I felt her swift, appraising glance. By that straight-through look I knew that Mrs. Eddy had read my thought and had taken my measure.

"This is indeed a privilege I have often wished for but never really expected to have," I said, "and I have brought you a little souvenir." It was indeed a *little* souvenir, nothing more than a memorandum book which my firm was distributing to customers. Mrs. Eddy accepted it as graciously as if it were a costly gift. Then, to my surprise, she turned to her maid saying, "Lydia, have you that little box I asked you to bring?"

"Here it is, Mother," she replied.

Mrs. Eddy handed me the box saying, "And I have brought you something." I opened the box and there was one of the silver souvenir spoons which had been made available to Christian Scientists the previous December.* These spoons bear a motto, "Not matter but Mind satisfieth," and to this motto is attached a story related to me by Calvin A. Frye, Mrs. Eddy's long-standing faithful secretary.

Early one cold winter morning in 1898, Mrs. Eddy called Mr. Frye and told him that during the night many wonderful thoughts had come to her. She talked about this for some time, then said, "Please write down this statement: Not matter but Mind satisfieth." Mr. Frye wrote the words on a slip of paper, but, he said, unlike his usual care in promptly filing all Mrs. Eddy's dictation, he laid the paper down and thought no more about it.

The following summer a proprietor of a silverware manufacturing firm and other Concord folk called on Mrs. Eddy one day seeking permission to produce a souvenir spoon. Mrs. Eddy was much interested. Suddenly she exclaimed, "Wait a moment. I

*Later Mrs. Eddy gave me one of these spoons in gold.

have just what is needed." Then she rang for Mr. Frye and asked him to bring her the slip of paper on which he had written the statement she had dictated to him during the winter.

Mr. Frye said that for a moment he was panic-stricken, for he realized that he had neglected to file that paper. He left the room not knowing where to look for it, but instantly the thought came: "Animal magnetism cannot make me the instrument for losing one word that God has given Mrs. Eddy. The same divine Mind that gave Mother that message protects it and will lead me to it." He was guided to go to the room where Mrs. Eddy had dictated the message and straight to the table drawer. There it was, the slip of paper with the message, "Not matter but Mind satisfieth," written in pencil. In telling this story Mr. Frye always added, "Mother never knew of the panic I was in when I could not recall where I had put that message!"

Of course I was delighted to receive this gift from Mrs. Eddy, and said, "I do thank you very much," adding frankly, "but I have one of these souvenir spoons already."

"Then you won't want this one," Mrs. Eddy said with a smile.

"Oh, yes, indeed I will, and I thank you very much," I hastened to assure her as I put the little box in my pocket. We all smiled broadly. We seemed very much like a large happy family.

I then proceeded to show the carpet samples, and Mrs. Eddy requested each one present whose room was to be recarpeted, to make his or her selection.

"Laura, choose what you would like for your room," she said, turning to Mrs. Sargent.

"You choose for me, Mother," Mrs. Sargent replied.

"Calvin, make your selection," she said to Mr. Frye.

"No, Mother, you make it," he responded.

Mrs. Eddy went through the same procedure with each one present. Frequently she turned to me saying, "What would be your choice, Mr. Hill?"

Each time I would answer, "I should choose the one I like

best, Mother," and Mrs. Eddy would say, "That is exactly what I shall do."

After I had stated three or four times that I should choose the carpet that I liked best, Mrs. Eddy shook her finger at me, saying, "But you have not yet said which one *you* would choose."

At that moment I learned that Mrs. Eddy did not like evasive answers; she liked positiveness. She had asked me a straightforward question which called for a straightforward answer, and I, unhesitatingly, gave her a very frank reply which was about as follows:

"In your front parlor, Mrs. Eddy, you have very fine Brussels net curtains, beautifully upholstered chairs, and a couch with a delicate covering; but in this rear parlor you have black walnut furniture with portieres and wallpaper which do not go together very well. A fine quality plain carpet, green or old rose, would look well in these double parlors. On the walls you should have the best paper that money can buy, and it would also be nice to have new window curtains."

With intensity I added: "One who has done so much for humanity should have the best of everything. Nothing is too good for you."

I was gesticulating as I talked, and Mrs. Eddy's alert gaze followed wherever I pointed. When I finished speaking she gently replied, "You know I do not go shopping very often so that I do not know much about the styles."

Of course I did not intend to be critical of Mrs. Eddy's home, which was in shining order. But I felt it was only right to give an honest opinion when she had asked for it, and I expressed myself as best I could. Later I had the privilege of helping Mrs. Eddy in the work of redecoration.

After we had finished selecting the carpets, Mrs. Eddy's thought quickly turned from the problems of her household to her larger household, the Cause.

Turning to me she said suddenly, "Have you seen the little

heart?" Not knowing what she meant, I shook my head. "You must come to my study and see it," she said emphatically.

I followed her to the foot of the stairs, and she motioned me to precede her. I hurried up expecting her to follow more slowly. However, when I reached the top of the stairs she was right behind me. The newspapers were constantly referring to Mrs. Eddy's age; she was at this time in her seventy-eighth year. I realized that I had unwittingly accepted the suggestion of waning strength, but none was apparent. Leading to a door, she stood aside while I opened it for her, and we entered her study, the room over the back parlor.

In the center of the room stood an oak table and on it an inverted glass bowl. Under this I saw a piece of paper on which was glued a rubber band in the shape of a heart. After we were seated, Mrs. Eddy related to me what that rubber band, forming a heart, meant to her.

I was able to follow her explanation in a measure, because I knew that at this time an attempt was being made by some of her students who did not understand her to discredit her as Leader. It was a crucial hour for the Cause.

Mrs. Eddy told me that one night when she was waiting on God for a message concerning this problem, she took up a sheaf of papers to look through them, and put on her wrist the rubber band that bound them. Later, as she was pacing the floor in prayer, she tossed the rubber band on a chest of drawers. She noticed that it fell in the exact shape of a heart.

It was characteristic of Mrs. Eddy to find "sermons in stones," and the smile of God in a rose. This shape of a heart which a rubber band sometimes takes symbolized for her, in that trying moment, the great heart of God, "the ever-presence of ministering Love" (*Science and Health,* p. 567). She was assured that God had guided her to a right decision and that His plan would prevail, and she was comforted. Immediately she sat down and wrote this beautiful poem, "Signs of the Heart," which closes with a prayer that the "barren brood" might be awakened to the joy of each finding his own God-appointed place and that the dove of peace might rest and abide with them all.

SIGNS OF THE HEART

Come to me, joys of heaven!
   Breathe through the summer air
A balm—the long-lost leaven
   Dissolving death, despair!
     O little heart,
     To me thou art
A sign that never can depart.

Come to me, peace on earth!
   From out life's billowy sea,—
A wave of welcome birth,—
   The Life that lives in Thee!
     O Love divine,
     This heart of Thine
Is all I need to comfort mine.

Come when the shadows fall,
   And night grows deeply dark;
The barren brood, O call
   With song of morning lark;
     And from above,
     Dear heart of Love,
Send us thy white-winged dove.

This poem written in April 1899, appeared in *The Christian Science Journal* of July 1899. Later it was included in her published poems (*Poems,* p. 24).

That our Leader's prayer was answered is attested by a letter from the First Members of The Mother Church written June the third, and printed in the same issue of *The Christian Science Journal* in which the poem appeared. This letter shows clearly that these students understood the symbolism of the heart. It read as follows:

To our beloved Mother in Israel:—

The First Members of the Mother Church in Semi-Annual Meeting assembled, thanking God that among the countless blessings bestowed upon us out of the rich storehouse of Infinite Love, we *know* that in you, our Leader, Guide, Friend, Counsellor, and Mother, we have our crowning blessing; because through you He has taught us of Himself—eternal Life and Love.

We desire, as best we know how, to express our deep and renewed appreciation of the wisdom, strength, and majesty of Truth as reflected through you, and the infinite tenderness of that love which bears and forbears, in its Christly purpose to redeem and save.

We desire, also, here and now, to place ourselves anew upon the altar of self-sacrifice on behalf of our sacred Cause, and to extend our deepest assurances of unflinching desire and purpose to support you in every way possible to us in this, your hour of seeming persecution, *but of great blessing.*

As "them of old time" were guided, encouraged, and uplifted by trope, metaphor, and symbol, so are you, in this age, being shown the way whereby you and your children are drawn by the *band* of unity into the great *Heart* of Love.

We once again assure you of our supreme desire to love God and one another. We feel that persecution is but driving us nearer to God and to each other; and that the only *real* effect of malicious attack is to strengthen our courage and faith.

We know that you dwell constantly in the secret place

of the Most High, because we believe the promises of God, and that "No weapon that is formed against thee shall prosper; and every tongue that shall rise against thee in judgment thou shalt condemn. This is the heritage of the servants of the Lord, and their right-eousness is of me, saith the Lord."

Your loving children,

The First Members of the Mother Church
Boston, Mass., June 3, 1899.

The insight into Mrs. Eddy's problems as Founder and Leader of the Christian Science movement, and her way of solving these problems as it was shown to me in her explanation of "Signs of the Heart," touched me deeply. As she continued talking of ever-present Love, my thought was lifted into the upper chamber of Spirit's reality and allness through the door of spiritual illumina-tion—understanding.

She then asked me many questions, evidently testing my grasp of Christian Science. My answers were based on what I had gleaned from her writings. Finally in a flash of apparent satisfac-tion with one of my answers, she said, "By the way, who is your teacher?"

"Well, Mrs.—— Mother,"* I replied, "I believe I shall have to call you my teacher. I have been studying your book, *Science and Health,* and your other writings for the past four years, and if what is said to me by one of your own students or by one of your students' students is not backed up or verified by your writings, I take no stock in his statements, none whatever!"

---

*Mrs. Eddy was called "Mother" by students and members of her household at that time. So it was quite natural for me, hearing "Mother" so often that day, to use the same term at our very first meeting. I can honestly say that I have always thought of her as Mother, from the first day I met her. Later Mrs. Eddy asked the students of Christian Science to discontinue calling her Mother.

Mrs. Eddy stepped forward, placed her hand on my shoulder and patted it gently, saying, "My child, my child, my child, you're safe, you're safe, you're safe!"

As I saw it then and as I understand it more fully now, Mrs. Eddy meant that one is safe as long as he depends solely on divine Principle as revealed in her writings. She then asked: "Why didn't I know you when I taught my last class? I would have had you in it." Pausing a moment she continued, "But it was a Normal class." With a smile, a twinkle in her eye, and a decisive shake of her head, she concluded, "But I would have had you ready!"

I have no doubt that Mrs. Eddy discerned my honesty of purpose, my sincere desire to do my part with her guidance to help her and the Cause.

She then inquired if I had any questions I wished to ask her, but I was so impressed with her purity and greatness and my own impurity and unworthiness and I was so filled with emotion that the tears were running down my cheeks, and I could only reply in a trembling voice, "No, Mother." I was aware that I was in the presence of the Discoverer and Founder of Christian Science— the woman who, like Jesus, perceived the reality and allness of Spirit and the utter unreality and nothingness of matter, and who brought to mankind the Comforter of which he spoke.

Concerning this, Mrs. Eddy writes in her textbook, *Science and Health with Key to the Scriptures* (p. 55):

> In the words of St. John: "He shall give you another Comforter, that he may abide with you *forever.*" This Comforter I understand to be Divine Science.

Of her inseparability from Christian Science, she has given us this explanation in *Miscellaneous Writings* (p. 105):

> Christian Science is my only ideal; and the individual and his ideal can never be severed. If either is misunder-

stood or maligned, it eclipses the other with the shadow cast by this error.

Mrs. Eddy then asked me if I had ever seen where she was born and led me out on the rear veranda which ran the full width of the house. Pointing straight ahead she said, "Right over that big tree, in the distance, are the Bow Hills where they say I was born." She paused and looked at me, or rather looked through me with that searching gaze which I later came to know so well. Then, instantly directing thought to man's spiritual nature and origin, she added, as I recall it, "But I wasn't, I was born in Mind." The gaze which followed that statement made an impression on me which can never be erased. I realized that she was speaking of her immortal, spiritual identity—that identity to which she clearly pointed in a letter written several years later to a clergyman:

> Should I give myself the pleasant pastime of seeing your personal self, or give you the opportunity of seeing mine, you would not see me thus, for I am not there. I have risen to look and wait and watch and pray for the spirit of Truth that leadeth away from person— from body to Soul, even to the true image and likeness of God. St. John found Christ, Truth, in the Word which *is* God. We look for the sainted Revelator in his writings, and there we find him. Those who look for me in person, or elsewhere than in my writings, lose me instead of find me (*The First Church of Christ, Scientist, and Miscellany*, pp. 119–120).

As we were returning to her study I said, "There *is* a question I should like to ask you, Mother." She turned to me at once saying eagerly, "What is it, dear?"

Calvin Frye, who had joined us, said, "Be seated, Mother; be seated, Mr. Hill." In a few moments he withdrew and Mrs. Eddy again looked at me searchingly as I put my question.

"I wish you would point me to some place in your book that will enable me to overcome the thought of lust and sensuality." She replied most emphatically, "I will!"

I remember she lifted her head with that far-off look, as though she saw into the very heart of heaven. She talked for some time denouncing the Adam-dream and thoroughly exposing its falsity. She spoke over and over again of the nothingness of mortality and of the reality of the spiritual creation. She supplanted the garment of flesh with the robe of Spirit. The light which dawned upon me that day has dwelt with me in greater or lesser degree ever since and has enabled me to understand her revelation better as the years pass. She talked as long as I could follow her; but when she saw that her statements were beyond what I was capable of understanding, extending her hand, she said quietly, "That will be all today, dear." This characteristic gesture, concluding our interview when I had ceased to follow her explanations, was to become very familiar in the near future.

As I left Pleasant View to return to the depot, after this memorable and uplifting experience, I felt as if I were walking on air. Nothing seemed real except the truth which Mrs. Eddy had affirmed and which was inscribed on the disc of my consciousness. People were passing in different directions, both on foot and in carriages, but I was scarcely aware of them—they seemed to be moving in a mist.

I boarded the train for Boston, and as I rode along, my thought was completely occupied with the great illumination of the reality of Spirit and the nothingness of matter. I felt that I had been lifted to the mount of transfiguration. For a number of days all I could think of, all I could hear, was what Mrs. Eddy had said to me in answer to my question, and the spiritual light which I received during that interview remained with me in all its glory.

From that time I was a different man; hence I feel warranted in saying that I experienced a measure of spiritual "new birth" on that wonderful day. However, later I had to learn that being lifted up by another, even by our Leader, is not working out one's own salvation; which is to say that there is no vicarious atonement. I saw that I had to work my own way up the hill of Science, that I had to prove in my own experience the truth she had affirmed to me,—I had to work it out in demonstration.

A month later I received a letter from Mr. Frye in which he said that he did not know why Mother requested it, but that she said to ask me to look on page 95, second paragraph, of *Science and Health*. In the fifty-fifth edition, 1891, then current, this read as follows:

> The devotion of mortal mind to some achievement makes its accomplishment possible. Exceptions only confirm this rule, proving that failure is occasioned by a too feeble sense of power.

In the final edition of the textbook, page 199, these lines were changed to read:

> The devotion of thought to an honest achievement makes the achievement possible. Exceptions only confirm this rule, proving that failure is occasioned by a too feeble faith.

From Mr. Frye's letter I understood that Mrs. Eddy was continuing to help me along the road in Christian Science. The following letter from her shows that she remembered my first interview with her and that she was eager to give me further light on a problem which everyone must meet and master:

> Goodness such as yours is a sure pre-text of success in all struggles to be "better." If a single sin remains— and who is destitute of all sin—be of good cheer

for the victory over it is a foregone conclusion. If a supposed sensation exists that God, Good, is displeased with it must yield and neither fear nor abnormal conditions can hold it. Your good heart is the victor over it and *now* and for ever you know this is truth and the Truth has made you *free*. You are liberated by divine Love from every false claim of the flesh. The law of Spirit is supreme, it dominates the flesh and you are God's own child. *Never* born of the flesh nor subject to it.

Here you plant your understanding and having done your part, *stand* and God will provide for the temptation strength to overcome it.

About a month after my first interview I had the privilege of a second interview with Mrs. Eddy, when I was in Concord on a short vacation. I was staying at the cottage on the Pleasant View estate with Joseph Mann and his sister Pauline, with whom I had lived in Boston. I noticed that some of the workers on the estate were trying to burn a huge pile of brush, mostly apple tree prunings, but they had poured kerosene on the branches without having built a good foundation and the green stuff would not burn.

Recalling how I had seen it done on my father's farm when I was a boy, I said laughingly, "Let me show you how to burn brush." The task was willingly turned over to me. I borrowed a pair of overalls and a work shirt and set about laying a good foundation of dry pieces. Soon the flames were leaping up. In the midst of this burning of brush, Pauline called to me from the cottage window, "Mr. Hill, Mother wants to see you right away."

I hurriedly washed up, changed into my own clothes and went to the house. Mrs. Eddy was awaiting me in the library. She greeted me graciously and motioned for me to be seated. As I did so I began twirling the end of my moustache excitedly, wondering what she was going to say to me. "Mr. Hill, what a pretty moustache you have," she remarked, perhaps desiring to put me at ease. She then came directly to the purpose of the interview.

"How are you getting along with that problem you asked me about when you were here last?"

"Mother," I replied, "I am not quite sure I understand just what you meant in your letter."

"What don't you understand, dear?"

"Well," I said, "you reminded me of your statement that 'the devotion of mortal mind to some achievement makes its accomplishment possible.' By this I understand that if one devotes his thought to any particular line of work he will accomplish something. But the second part of the citation, 'Exceptions only confirm this rule, proving that failure is occasioned by a too feeble sense of power,' I don't know that I understand this. Does it mean my too feeble sense of power in Christian Science?"

"You *do* understand! That is exactly what it means," Mrs. Eddy replied emphatically. At that moment I awakened as I had not before to realization of the spiritual power of the statements of scientific truth in Christian Science.

Mrs. Eddy then began to explain a number of important points in the teaching and practice of Christian Science. She talked for fully half an hour and again I felt the inspiration of her spirituality.

This second exalting experience, following so closely upon the first one, seemed a wonderful climax to my four years of earnest study of the Bible and Mrs. Eddy's writings. My gratitude for Christian Science and to its Leader was so deep that I longed to serve her and the Cause in every way possible.

I consider that the opportunities that almost immediately began to come to me were the outcome of my sincere desire to give my life to the Cause of Christian Science, and of my firm conviction of its healing power.

When I was living with Joseph Mann and his sister in Boston, before they moved to Pleasant View, Joseph told me of his first healing in Christian Science. Owing to the fact that it was so valuable to me as evidence of the power of Truth and also because of Mrs. Eddy's personal interest in the case, I here give the account of it.

This healing was widely known at the time it occurred because it had been presented at a hearing of a Committee of Doctors and Druggists which was attempting, through legislation, to prevent the practice of Christian Science healing. The National Constitutional Liberty League of Boston and New York published a pamphlet which included "The Christian Science Case" as prepared by Judge Septimus J. Hanna, then Editor of *The Christian Science Journal.* In this report Joseph Mann's testimony appeared as follows:

"AFFIDAVIT.
"Commonwealth of Massachusetts,)
              County of Suffolk.) ss.
"Joseph G. Mann, being duly sworn, on his oath states:
"In November, 1886, I was accidentally shot with a thirty-two calibre revolver, the ball entering the left breast near the nipple. I immediately became unconscious, was carried into the house and laid on the nearest bed. On our doctor's arrival the family were informed that I had received a fatal wound; indeed so serious did he consider the case that he felt unwilling to father its responsibility alone. Accordingly three more well known and eminent physicians were summoned post haste. One of these was known in the city whence he came as a skillful surgeon. All four are today in the field of practice and their standing is considered as good as any in the medical profession, and in the community in which they live they are known as honest men. They examined the wound closely and carefully and concluded it would be useless to probe for the ball for if they should attempt this, or in any way stir me, I would die on their hands. They further concluded, that judging from the excessive bleeding, both internally and externally, and the peculiar color of the blood, the ball had touched the heart, and was probably lodged in the pericardium.

"The doctors informed the family that they were unable to

stop the flow of blood, and should they attempt this from without, I would still bleed inwardly, and thus bleed to death.

"After a few hours they held a council in an adjoining room, and then told the family there was no hope, saying to father: 'Mr. Mann, we are sorry, but we can do nothing for your son.' In his sorrow and desperation father implored them to spare nothing that money might afford, send for any other help that might bring hope; but they said it would be useless.

"With this verdict the three departed. While our family physician still lingered he kept the family informed that I was gradually dying; the body was growing cold, and before he left the house the eyes were becoming set and the death perspiration stood on the forehead. As he went out he said to our grieving friends that death was so near, the pulse was scarcely perceptible. All human help had now left, and the last hope of the family went out with it. So sure were the doctors of my death that they themselves told our friends and relatives, by the way, that they would never see me again alive. Telegrams were written and held ready to spread the news that I was dead.

"In this last moment, Christian Science was providentially brought to our door. The family had never heard of this (to them) new method of healing and refused to admit the Scientist; for, as they said, they wanted no one to experiment on the dying whom the *doctors* had given up as hopeless.

"They were assured, however, that the patient should not be touched or given medicine; and that 'man's extremity has been (is) God's opportunity.' Within about fifteen minutes after Christian Science had been admitted into our house I began suddenly to grow warm again under its treatment. My breath was again revived and normal. I became conscious, opened my eyes and knew I should not die, but would live. That same evening I sat up in bed and ate a little steak and toast. The excruciating pain I had felt during intervals of consciousness while dying, was all gone and I was steadily and rapidly growing strong and well. Notwithstanding the great loss of blood, I was strong enough the next day to have my blood-saturated garments (which had dried during the night and had to be removed by cutting) exchanged for clean ones. Beyond washing the wound and body to cleanse them from the blood, no attention was given them. The doctors on hearing that I had not died, predicted that gangrene and other evils would yet set in, especially on account of the excessive internal bleeding, and this would certainly produce death. I however continued to improve. The same power that had brought me to this point of recovery, forestalled also the bad results which the M.D.'s expected. The second day I was out of bed and dressed the greater part of the time; and the third day found me up bright and early and about with the family as though the accident had never occurred.

"That our mourning had been turned into joy is true, indeed; and to prove to my many visitors that I was really healed and quite like myself again in so short a time, I took my part with the family in singing our familiar church hymns; all were agreed that my voice was strong and sound. Relatives who had come to attend the funeral rejoiced with me instead. The wound healed inwardly and outwardly without any apparent inflammation, swelling, or suppuration; and meanwhile, from the fourth day on, I walked out to visit friends, rode with the family in carriage and sleigh over rough roads, and in all kinds of weather without sustaining the slightest ill effects therefrom.

"Christian Science not only perfectly healed me after the medical doctors had failed and had given me up, but through what understanding I have gained, I have ever since been kept well. When I was first healed I experienced a little soreness during the first few weeks of my being about, but this soon entirely disappeared, and not a sensation from the wound have I felt since.

"In the village which bears witness to my healing, is the home of my father, John F. Mann, where he has resided for upwards of forty years. I have no doubt that he, or any honest man, who was a citizen of Broad Brook, town of East Windsor, Hartford Co., Conn., where my healing occurred, will give his testimony to any reader who might wish further evidence than my statement of it.

"Any who would personally inquire into this case are kindly invited to call on me at 418 Columbus Avenue, Boston, Mass.

"Joseph G. Mann.

"Subscribed and sworn to before me this 27th day of February, A.D. 1894.
(Seal)   "Walter L. Church, *Notary Public.*"

At the time of the healing related in the foregoing affidavit, Mr. Mann was twenty-two years of age. When the physicians gave their verdict that death was inevitable, the grief of the family was intensified by the fact that it was a brother-in-law who had accidentally shot him when the two young men were target-practicing with thirty-two calibre revolvers. When life returned the joy of the family was correspondingly great, and their gratitude for healing in Christian Science was profound. It turned three brothers and two sisters to active interest in Christian Science.

The first thing Joseph Mann said when he returned to consciousness was, "Is this something I can learn, and do for others?"

He immediately began to study the Christian Science textbook, and many, upon hearing of his healing, went to him for help, and he healed them.

When Mrs. Eddy was informed of his healing work she invited him to attend her class, which he did in 1888. Shortly after, he established his practice in Boston, and his sister Pauline joined him to keep his home. Ten years later, hearing of Mrs. Eddy's need for an overseer on her Pleasant View estate, he volunteered his services and left a growing practice in order to help her. In this same year Mrs. Eddy invited him to be a member of her last class, the well-known "class of seventy."

One day, when Mrs. Eddy was having a conversation with Joseph Mann, she questioned him in detail about his remarkable experience and especially about the regeneration which took place in him while he stood in the vestibule of death, a change which had come of an experience almost equal to his having died and then been resurrected.

Mrs. Eddy summarized the incident conclusively, I was told, in these words: "Joseph, you have had a *wonderful* experience; you were thrown violently out of the house, and picked yourself up on the outside; go not back into it."

My service to Mrs. Eddy began with making purchases for her and for members of her household. Soon she was entrusting me with messages to her Board of Directors in Boston. Later I served as Assistant to this Board. From this work there unfolded to me the opportunity, under Mrs. Eddy's direction, to find and recommend Christian Scientists to serve as helpers in her home. In 1901 I was appointed by our Leader as a First Member. (In 1903 the name "First Member" was changed to "Executive Member" and so continued until that body was dissolved in 1908.) In 1902 by unanimous vote of The Christian Science Board of Directors I was elected Superintendent of The Mother Church Sunday School, which office I held for fourteen years. Upon recommendation of Mrs. Eddy, in December of the same year, the Directors appointed me a member of the Finance Committee of The Mother Church. I served on this Committee for almost forty years.

The demands on Mrs. Eddy were so many that at times several secretaries were required to care for the correspondence. Resident secretaries and other workers necessitated a large household staff. The work of cook, waitress, housemaid, laundress, seamstress, and personal maid had to be done by sincere, unselfish Christian Scientists. All of those who were called to Pleasant View and employed there were experienced workers in Christian Science. Many had been Readers in branch churches, and some were teachers and practitioners. It was an inestimable privilege to live at Pleasant View and to be under the instruction and supervision of their Leader. In this connection Mrs. Eddy wrote in the *Christian Science Sentinel* of April 25, 1903: "It is true that loyal Christian Scientists, called to the home of the Discoverer and Founder of

Christian Science, can acquire in one year the Science that other-wise might cost them a half century" (*Miscellany,* p. 229).

Nevertheless, it was a constant problem for Mrs. Eddy to keep the staff of helpers she needed. Some who began their work with inspiration found it difficult to retain their joy and spiritual vision, especially if their assigned work seemed to be menial. Others could not continue because of strong home ties or for other personal reasons.

For more than two years I was assigned the whole task of find-ing helpers for Pleasant View. Then a committee was formed for this purpose, and I became a member of this committee.

In connection with this work Mrs. Eddy told me that in my quest for helpers I should go first to her own students—those who had received class instruction from her. She said that if such were physically fit they were the ones to serve in her home, because she knew what God had planted in their thought through her teaching, and at the proper time she could awaken that and make use of it. She said, "Get one who loves to work for the Cause and is willing to take up the cross for it as I have done." I knew that the qualities of thought re-quired by our Leader in her helpers included love, orderliness, promptness, alertness, accuracy, truthfulness, fidelity, consecra-tion, and humility. Mrs. Eddy commended me when, in one of my interviews with her, I said: "Mother, in looking for helpers for you, I am not trying to find a pleasant personality. I am looking for a quality of thought that reflects the great revela-tion you have given to the world." In her personal interviews with prospective helpers, I have known many cases in which she clearly discerned their thought and character at the first meeting. This evidenced her understanding of divine Mind. Mrs. Eddy knew immediately whether or not a person could qualify for membership in her household. There was never any question about it. I learned that she was always right, whatever I myself may have thought about the adaptability of a candidate. As I saw her great intuition and wisdom manifested again and again I came to the conviction that her judgment was as near perfection as is possible in this world.

One day when I was with Mrs. Eddy she rang for her personal maid and requested that she bring some article to her. The maid returned, bringing something totally different from what Mrs. Eddy had asked for. Mrs. Eddy looked at her earnestly and said, "Dear, that isn't what I told you to bring; I told you to bring [naming the article], and I told you where to find it. Now please get it."

Turning to me Mrs. Eddy remarked, as I recall her words, "That is what animal magnetism does to the members of my household, and they will say, 'Mother sometimes forgets!' " A few moments later Mrs. Eddy's ability to read thought accurately was again made apparent, for shortly after I left her I met the same maid in the hall, and she said to me, "Mother sometimes forgets what she asks for!"

In a letter to me Mrs. Eddy wrote: "We never can know who is in reality a Christian Scientist until he is tested under fire; then what is left are dregs unfit for use till purged and purified or they are qualities that evil cannot destroy and are held by the power of God." She further explained that in some cases the residue was mere sensuous, self-blind human will, whereas only the very opposite of this constitutes the individual, much more the Christian Scientist.

On one occasion Mrs. Eddy said to me, in substance, "The first thing I do in the morning when I awake is to declare I shall have no other mind before divine Mind, and become fully conscious of this, and adhere to it throughout the entire day; then the evil cannot touch me." Many times she said to me, "All my hours are His."

Revealing the glory of her discovery, in a letter dated August 2, 1906, she wrote to me,

Pleasant View,
Concord, N.H.
Aug. 2, 1906.

Mother's darling:

If you know who that is then you will know why it is so. Your dear letter strengthens me. I am having much of the experience that you name but on an opposite basis utterly; "When first I learned my Lord" I was so sure of Truth, my faith so strong in Christian Science as I then discovered it, I had no struggle to meet; but stood on the height of its glory a crowned monarch triumphant over sin and death. But behold me now washing that spiritual understanding with my tears! Learning little by little the *allness* of Omnipotent Mind; and the nothingness of matter, yea the absolute nothingness of *nothing* and the infinite somethingness of ALL. O bear with me, loved one, till I accomplish the height, the depth, the Horeb light of divine Life,—divine Love, divine health, holiness and immortality. The way seems not only long but very strait and narrow. Lovingly in Christ Yours ever,—

Mary Baker Eddy

The work I was doing for Mrs. Eddy necessitated my being in frequent touch with her. Sometimes I saw her several times a week. On every occasion she expressed a loving interest in my welfare and gave a little of her valuable time to explain to me how to work in Christian Science. She read my thought as one reads an open book and discerned what I myself was unaware of, an unhealed fear of tuberculosis. She never talked to me of this, but in several of her letters to me she mentioned lungs. These excerpts were so helpful that I quote some of them in order that they may bless others.

In April 1907, she wrote: "Dear one, look on the cloud of lungs till you see the Father's face—the sense of life not in nor of matter and this spiritual recognition will destroy the cloud forever, it *will.*"

A few months later I received the following letter from her:

> Pleasant View,
> Concord, N.H.
> Nov. 9, 1907.
>
> My beloved: Read Science and Health page 188. ¶. 3. and may you get the meaning of what I said to you when last here.
>
> It seems to the material senses that pain etc. are in the lungs or elsewhere *in matter* but the fact is that pain or suffering of any sort is no more in the body or matter in our waking state than it is in our *night dream* for *both* states are *dreams* and not the reality of being.
>
> Lovingly yours,
> M B Eddy

The following spring, in a letter, thanking me for some specially fine strawberries I had sent her, she said: "May, O may the Love divine feed you and fill you with a strong sense of *liberty,* of waking from the dream of life in lungs—the Infinite in the finite—and show you just how a lie destroys itself by saying I am real!"

Mrs. Eddy was deeply interested in the spiritual progress of her helpers and placed great value on their practice of Christian Science healing. She once said to me, as I recall it: "Get your heart right with the heart of God. That is what heals the sick. Get right yourself. Now, you get a practice and know that it is not you that heals, but that it is getting right yourself."

When I told her that I had decided to give up business in order to devote all my time, apart from serving her and the Cause, to the practice, she wrote:

Pleasant View,
Concord, N.H.
March 2, 1903.

Beloved Student:

I am glad that you have left all, left but nothing for something, and this something *is All.*

God bless your brave, honest intent with its fullest fruition.

There are the sick the halt the blind to be healed. Is not this enough to be able to accomplish? Were I to name that which is most needed to be done of all else on earth—I should say heal the sick, cleanse the spotted despoiled mortal; and then you are being made whole and happy, and this is thine. "Well done good and faithful" enter thou into all worldly worth and the joy of thy Lord, the recompence of rightness. Again, God bless you, dear one, and guide your footsteps.

With love,
M B G Eddy

Those who served Mrs. Eddy were blessed by the lovely grace of gratitude which she expressed. Gratitude was inherent in her nature and it unfailingly blossomed in some gracious way, a gift or a priceless statement of Truth—often with a delightful flash of humor, for she had a keen sense of humor.

On one of my early visits to Pleasant View, I noticed the chair Mrs. Eddy used regularly, an armchair upholstered in gold plush, was badly worn, and decided to surprise her with a new one. I had exact measurements taken and a reproduction made. One day while Mrs. Eddy was taking her drive I removed the old chair and put the new one in its place. With this gift I left a letter saying, "This chair is given to Mother with a sense of love and gratitude which cannot be expressed in words and my only desire is that it may give you the comfort that it does me the joy in giving it." In closing I thanked her for all she had done for me and for all mankind by her work and words. This gift delighted Mrs. Eddy, and she sent me a letter in which she quoted these lines from Eliza Cook's "The Old Arm-Chair," a poem very well known at that particular time:

> I love it, I love it! and who shall dare
> To chide me for loving that old arm-chair?

Mrs. Eddy's study, Chestnut Hill

In this letter she enclosed a "card complimentary" to the Normal class of the Massachusetts Metaphysical College, which was to be held the following June.

This gift of a chair has a sequel. In 1907, when plans were being made for Mrs. Eddy's move from Pleasant View to Chestnut Hill, Massachusetts, one of my tasks was to have exact duplicates made of the oak furniture in her Pleasant View sitting room and bedroom. The reproductions were to be in mahogany, in light finish for the living room and in dark for her bedroom. One day when examining the furniture to be reproduced, I noted that the chair I had given to Mrs. Eddy in 1901 needed repairing and decided to have a duplicate of this made as a gift to her.

Recalling her letter of thanks in which she had quoted from "The Old Arm-Chair," I sent her the following note:

> I would not dare chide you for loving your old
> armchair, but I have had made a duplicate of it so that
> you will not be the least inconvenienced while
> it is being repaired and made comfortable for you; then
> this new one can be placed in your new home when
> ready to be used until the other one can be forwarded.
> It is with much love and gratitude, and a sense of
> indebtedness to you which can never be repaid, that
> I present this gift with the hope that it may
> give you as much comfort as any earthly thing
> possibly can.

In her letter of thanks Mrs. Eddy spoke of the depths of her lone heart which seldom had company, and again referred to the poem, "The Old Arm-Chair," quoting the line, "I've bedewed it with tears, I've embalmed it with sighs." With her never-failing humor she added, "not size!"

I sent a little dish which I thought would be useful for her luncheon tray, and the next day I received the following letter:

Pleasant View,
Concord, N.H.
March 10, 1905

My dear Student:

You are more than a hill—you are a mountain, and
the dwelling place of tenderness, unselfishness, Soul.
The silver dish you sent me is very convenient to keep
my lunch warm. Will you let me pay for it? I feel badly
to have you expend your money for me. It is all I need
and just what I do need to have you care for my needs,
just as you are doing. God bless you, dear one, fill
you with victory over the falsities of human thought
and with sweet peace and rest from all fear. *Love*
casts out fear.

Lovingly yours in Truth,
Mary Baker Eddy.

Perhaps one of the most useful little gifts I gave Mrs. Eddy was
a jewel box. She wrote me that it was always on her dressing case
and that the compartments told her just where all her different
things were to be found so that she could put her finger on them
in the dark. In thanking me she wrote, "Order is essential to me."
The letter closed with a benediction, "May heaven's rich blessings
fall upon you as gently as dew upon the flowers."

One day Mrs. Eddy asked me to purchase suitable envelopes for
her calling cards. She wrote on the back of one of the cards which
she gave me, this treasured message, "With love untold to my
faithful servant of God."

For the piazza at her Pleasant View home, I sent her a rubber
mat with the word "Eddy" worked into the design. In a letter acknowledging this she said, "Excuse my not knowing what to call
it." I replied, "Call that something on your doorstep a love gift
for Mother and you will have the right name for it."

Mrs. Eddy's overflowing gratitude to her helpers was often expressed in charming gifts which we all treasured. In 1904 she sent me a twenty-dollar gold piece dated 1861 and with this a small reproduction of a photograph of herself which I placed in a little leather case and carried in my vest pocket. In a letter accompanying these gifts she wrote, "Accept my golden gift as the symbol of your Golden Rule of life." In thanking her for these, I wrote, referring to the photograph: "I have a better picture of you though than this one. It is a mental picture and was obtained by studying your writings. My desire is that the sunlight of Truth may fully develop this picture in my consciousness."

The following year she gave me a beautiful gold locket set with a diamond, containing another photograph of herself. In acknowledging this I wrote in part:

> I wish you could have seen my joyful surprise when I opened the box and looked upon the two faces—both solitaires, one with the lustre of, and symbolic of the light of faith and hope, the guiding star which led the wise men to where Jesus lay. The other with the lustre of, and reflecting spiritual being, growing brighter and brighter unto the perfect day because looking steadfastly upon the face of God, divine Love, symbolic of the light within—"the true Light, which lighteth every man that cometh into the world." I shall often look upon this face which reflects the Christ, to bring to memory my best and dearest earthly friend, the one who has followed unswervingly in the Master's footsteps, that I may receive renewed courage to continue in the way.

Mrs. Eddy loved to give books and she gave me several which she autographed. Most treasured of all is my copy of her textbook, *Science and Health with Key to the Scriptures.*

In 1907 the so-called "Next Friends" launched a legal attack on Mrs. Eddy in an attempt to prove her incapable of taking care of her own affairs. Had these "Next Friends" succeeded in their purpose they would have obtained possession not only of her property but also of the copyright of *Science and Health*.

On March 24 of that year in a letter to me Mrs. Eddy said:

> My beloved Student:
>
> I beg that you will come to me March 26 or 27 to watch with me one or two weeks as the case may require.
>
> This hour is going to test Christian Scientists and the fate of our Cause and they must not be found wanting. They must forget self and remember only their God and their Wayshower and their duty to have one God and love their neighbor as themselves. I see this clearly that the prosperity of our Cause hangs in this balance. May God open your eyes to see this and to come to her who has borne for you the burden in the heat of the day.

Similarly she appointed others, until there were twelve of us who were asked to do special work.

During the progress of the trial, I went to Pleasant View daily after each court session, carrying word to Mrs. Eddy from her chief legal counsel, "General" Streeter, as to the progress of the case. She always received me at once, apparently waiting for me to come from the courtroom. I have a vivid picture of her, sitting quietly and listening to what I had to report. She reminded me of a gray gull riding calmly, serenely, on a storm-tossed sea. She had full confidence in the triumph of Truth in this trial. As I recall, she once said to me, "You cannot hurt anyone by telling the truth, and no one can hurt you by telling a lie."

Of course I remember best of all the eventful day when I hurried out to Pleasant View and told her that the legal battle was ended—and that she had won. When she heard this she raised her hands from the arms of her chair and dropped them again, she lifted her head—a movement which had become familiar to all of us when she was doing metaphysical work or when she was deeply moved. Her eyes had a far-off look as if she were seeing the very heart of heaven.

Almost at once she turned to her desk and wrote for a few minutes. It was a letter of overflowing forgiveness to one of those in whose name the suit had been brought. I thought of Jesus' words, "Father, forgive them; for they know not what they do."

For my work in connection with this case Mrs. Eddy gave me directions which I immediately wrote down. She wanted the belief of "lawsuit" handled with absolute metaphysics. I was not to outline what the verdict would be but to know that Truth would prevail and that divine Mind would direct the verdict—which it certainly did.

My mental work was based on the Daily Prayer in the *Manual* and also on Article VIII, Section 6, "Alertness to Duty." Mrs. Eddy pointed out the need for specifically handling hypnotism in this case. She quoted from the Bible: "Shall not the Judge of all the earth do right?" (Genesis 18:25), "Surely the wrath of man shall praise thee: the remainder of wrath shalt thou restrain" (Psalm 76:10), and "We know that all things work together for good to them that love God" (Romans 8:28). In every detail her instruction was Christianly scientific.

Illustrating once more her ready wit, Mrs. Eddy wrote me shortly before the suit was won and signed her letter, "Your best friend but not your 'next friend.'"

Many times I have been asked to describe Mrs. Eddy. I recall her graceful form, her small hands and feet, her delicate rose coloring and white hair expressing the charm of a Dresden figure. Her face was almost unwrinkled, but there were crinkly lines of humor at the corners of her eyes. Her mouth showed firmness, but her smile was inexpressibly sweet. Her eyes were wonderful —deep, searching, far-seeing, but with often a merry twinkle. Her expression responded instantly to her thought. She had a quick sense of humor and in the midst of serious business had time for a word of wit or enjoyment of an amusing situation.

When those of us who were associated with Mrs. Eddy have given our recollections of her as a "corporeal person" (*Miscellaneous Writings,* p. 152), we come back to the fact that she can be truly known only through her work for God and humanity. She discovered the Science of Being. She proved it in healing and so made it practical for mankind. She systematized its teaching and so made it universally available. She gave the *Church Manual* and thereby made her church secure against "the sacrilegious moth of time" (*Miscellany,* p. 230); she established this "eternal Science" as a "permanent dispensation" (*Science and Health,* p. 150).

Under the caption "Practise the Golden Rule" Mrs. Eddy wrote to the *Boston Globe* in 1905, "Through the wholesome chastisements of Love, nations are helped onward towards justice, righteousness, and peace, which are the landmarks of prosperity." And as though summarizing her own immortal achievement she adds, "In order to apprehend more, we must practise what we already know of the Golden Rule, which is to all mankind a light emitting light" (*Miscellany,* p. 282).

Through Mary Baker Eddy, God has given to humanity the complete, final revelation of Truth, divine Science.

Impressions of Our Leader

BLISS KNAPP

J ohn the Baptist was quick to recognize Jesus as the Lamb of God, because John was a spiritual seer. But when the chief priests and elders asked Jesus by what authority he did his mighty works, "Jesus answered . . . The baptism of John, whence was it? from heaven, or of men? And they reasoned with themselves, saying, If we shall say, From heaven; he will say unto us, Why did ye not then believe him? But if we shall say, Of men; we fear the people; for all hold John as a prophet. And they answered Jesus, and said, We cannot tell. And he said unto them, Neither tell I you by what authority I do these things" (Matthew 21:24–27). Jesus knew that spiritual things must be spiritually discerned, and he had the wisdom to let his heaven-bestowed authority remain a mystery to them.

The crucifixion of Jesus caused the world to doubt his teachings. When he came victoriously out of the tomb, he discovered that two of his disciples were questioning his Messiahship while on their way to Emmaus. Seeing the need of defending his ministry, he "drew near, and went with them. . . . And beginning at Moses and all the prophets, he expounded unto them in all the scriptures the things concerning himself" (Luke 24:15, 27). He knew where those prophetic references were in the Old Testament writings, and he explained their application to himself. When the disciples' eyes were opened, and they saw their Master's true identity in Biblical prophecy, that spiritual comprehension of Jesus' place in prophecy closed their minds to any further disloyalty.

Whether we know it or not, we today are being tested in regard to the teachings of Mary Baker Eddy. Are they from heaven, or of men? Those who think of her as just the daughter of Mark Baker might regard her as only another religious leader; but Mrs. Eddy explained her own place in Biblical prophecy, even as Jesus had explained his place in prophecy on the way to Emmaus.

We are familiar with Mrs. Eddy's statement (*Miscellany*, p. 120), "Those who look for me in person, or elsewhere than in my writings, lose me instead of find me." But she also says (*ibid.*, p. 133), "My book is not all you know of me." And why? Because the remainder of what we can know of her true selfhood must be found in the Bible, in both the Old and the New Testament. That is why the Bible Lesson Committee is never at a loss to find suitable references in the Bible for the lesson on Christian Science. Mrs. Eddy has said (*ibid.*, p. 143), "It is self-evident that the discoverer of an eternal truth cannot be a temporal fraud."

My father and mother were among Mrs. Eddy's early students. When they first took class instruction with her, Mrs. Eddy had not yet included in *Science and Health* her explanation of the twelfth chapter of the book of Revelation. However, she gave an oral explanation of that chapter to the class. The first verse reads as follows: "And there appeared a great wonder in heaven; a woman clothed with the sun, and the moon under her feet, and upon her head a crown of twelve stars." As my father sat there listening to her explanation of that scriptural verse, he exclaimed, "Thou art the woman." By this is meant that Mrs. Eddy, in her human experience, represented the woman of the Apocalypse, for as Mrs. Eddy states in *Science and Health* (p. 565) the Christ-idea was "represented first by man and, according to the Revelator, last by woman."

I shall always remember my first meeting with Mrs. Eddy. It was when she came to spend a few days in our home. I was a very shy lad, especially at the approach of strangers; but Mrs. Eddy's love was so apparent that it melted all my shyness from the first moment that I saw her. We had some baby chicks at the time, and I thought it would interest her to see one, and it did. When I placed that little chicken in her hands, she seemed very much pleased, and talked to me about my pets. This incident must have impressed her in some way, because she remembered it and sometimes told the members of her household about it. She even recalled it to me more than once in later years. From the time of that introduction, Mrs. Eddy gained my absolute confidence and trust. It was just as natural for me to seek her counsel and advice as it was for me to take my problems to my mother, and she invariably gave my questions her loving consideration.

I shall always remember another incident during Mrs. Eddy's visit to our home. She had been awake all night in prayer over some problem, and had not gained her peace with the coming of dawn. Just before breakfast, my sister sat down at the organ and began to play and sing that old gospel hymn, "Joy cometh in the morning." My father, who was a member of the local church choir, joined in the singing, and they sang with such spirit that Mrs. Eddy came out of her room with a radiant face; the song had brought her refreshment and an answer to her prayers. She remembered this incident also, for she wrote to my father, "Sing again the old sacred song referred to on the first page of this letter—and sing it in the spirit you had in N. Hampshire when you sung it *years ago.*" Part of that hymn is now included in our *Christian Science Hymnal,* as Hymn No. 425.

Calvin Frye once laughingly told me how he tried to dissuade Mrs. Eddy from appointing me to the Board of Lectureship by reminding her of my extreme shyness and inexperience. He even told her she was making a mistake, but she brushed his advice aside and made the appointment. In addition to her prayers for me, she sent me a little book on elocution, and edited my first lecture in her own handwriting. When she returned my lecture, she wrote a comforting and helpful letter which wrought wonders in carrying me through that critical period of learning how to meet public criticism.

One time when my father had to see Mrs. Eddy on some church matters, he took me with him. It was a hot summer's day, and we walked out to Pleasant View. When we arrived,

Mrs. Eddy noticed that I was perspiring, and she asked if I would like a fan. Her question embarrassed me somewhat, and I declined with thanks. However, she insisted that I should have a special fan, which she asked Calvin Frye to bring her. While he was getting the fan, Mrs. Eddy told me a most interesting story about it. A former slave in the southland had made it of turkey feathers, and it was presented to Mrs. Eddy by a dear friend in gratitude and remembrance. Evidently the fan meant a great deal to her, for she talked about it so much; and I began to sense that she was trying to teach me some lesson by means of it. When Mr. Frye finally handed me the fan, I began to examine it as an object of interest. Then Mrs. Eddy said, "I want you to use that fan." Obediently, I began to use it in the natural way, and then she took my father into another room for a private conference.

On the way back to the hotel, I began to wonder if there could be any reference to a fan in the Glossary to *Science and Health*. To my joy, I found the following definition (p. 586): "FAN. Separator of fable from fact; that which gives action to thought." Not fully satisfied, I consulted the Concordance to *Science and Health,* as soon as I reached home, and found this reference on page 466: "The Science of Christianity comes with fan in hand to separate the chaff from the wheat."

We should remember that John the Baptist came with "fan in hand," and this "separator of fable from fact" enabled him to see Jesus as the Lamb of God.

In these days of world revolution, when there is so much mental confusion, we all need that "separator of fable from fact"; and we shall be most secure if we approach all our problems with "fan in hand."

Some time after that experience with the fan, I began to recall a story which I used to read in school; it was the story of the Key Flower by Bayard Taylor, which is in *Swinton's Fourth Reader.* I was so impressed by the story that I finally wrote a summary of it to Mrs. Eddy, and drew from it a certain analogy to her. I am sure you will be glad to hear the story and her response to it.

Briefly the story is as follows. One summer's day a shepherd was tending his sheep, when he discovered an unusual flower. As he picked it for closer examination, he noticed a door in the side of the mountain. It was strange that he had never noticed it before; but there it was, and it was open. Cautiously passing along a corridor, he entered a large room filled with chests of gold and diamonds. Then he saw, seated in a chair, an old dwarf with a long beard. The dwarf greeted him kindly and said, "Take what you want, and don't forget the best."

Placing the flower on the table, the shepherd proceeded to fill his pockets and hat with the gold and diamonds. Occasionally the old dwarf would remind him not to forget the best. When the shepherd could carry no more, he turned to leave. On reaching the door, he heard the voice for the last time crying out, "Don't forget the best." The next minute the shepherd was out in the pasture. As he looked around, the door had vanished; his pockets and hat had grown light all at once, and instead of gold and diamonds, he found nothing but dry leaves and pebbles. He was as poor as ever, because he had forgotten the best. The flower which he had left on the table in the dwarf's room was the Key Flower, and had he kept it, the gold and diamonds would have stayed so, and the door of the treasure room would have been open to him whenever he might wish to enter.

I told Mrs. Eddy that she is our Key Flower. She has unlocked the treasures of heaven; and no one knows anything of Christian Science except as it has come through her. If we wish those heavenly treasures to remain real and demonstrable, we must never permit our Leader to be separated in our thought from her teachings.

Her letter in response is in part as follows: "Your story and its semblance are sweeter than birds and blossoms that I long for; and to think that you love God, and love me by way of remembrance and fidelity, fills my lone heart, feeds my hungry sense of nothing, with home and Heaven.

"I wish I could do more for you, but that is selfish for it would give me much pleasure. Let me wish only that my prayers for you are righteous, then I know the result will rest in sweet hope of your prosperity, growth in grace, and the knowledge of infinite Love, where no arrow wounds the dove, where are no partings, no pain."

Today people are greatly troubled over world conditions. We are taught in Christian Science that such conflicting forces indicate the breaking up of mortal mind's long-cherished beliefs, and we can rejoice at the overturning of error. But Jesus said of such conditions (Matthew 24:12), "Because iniquity shall abound, the love of many shall wax cold." This is a warning not to forget the best. Let us watch and pray that we be not made to forget nor to neglect our Leader—our Key Flower, who has unlocked for us the treasures of heaven. As St. John has said (Revelation 3:11), "Hold that fast which thou hast, that no man take thy crown."

"With sandals on and staff in hand"

CLARA KNOX McKEE

*I*t is a great privilege to write about our dear Leader, Mary Baker Eddy, whom I had the opportunity of knowing personally and serving at Pleasant View during one of the greatest trials of her life. I was called to Pleasant View in August 1906. Several months later there was filed in the New Hampshire Court the so-called "Next Friends" suit which was brought against her, to deprive her of the management of her property. This trial lasted until August 21, 1907, when the so-called "Next Friends" and their attorneys were forced to admit that they could not sustain any of the charges in their petition, and thereupon filed a motion for dismissal of the suit.

If you could have known our Leader at that time, you would have realized that she was in the arms of divine Love. While doing everything necessary to defend herself and her publications, she went right on with her daily duties and her writing, thus magnificently fulfilling her own words, "As of old, I stand with sandals on and staff in hand, waiting for the watchword and the revelation of what, how, whither" (*Miscellaneous Writings,* p. 158).

At that time, she was revising *Science and Health with Key to the Scriptures.* She had a copy of the three-dollar edition taken apart in sections; this was placed right side up in the left-hand side of her desk drawer. She would take off one section at a time and go through it. Then that one was placed upside down in the right-hand side of the drawer. When she had finished going over every page of the entire book, it was in perfect order.

In *Miscellaneous Writings* (p. 311) our Leader says, "The works I have written on Christian Science contain absolute Truth, and my necessity was to tell it; . . . I was a scribe under orders; . . ." Again in *The First Church of Christ, Scientist, and Miscellany* she writes (pp. 251–252), "Adhere to the teachings of the Bible, Science and Health, and our Manual, and you will obey the law and gospel. Have one God and you will have no devil."

The Christian Science Journal was our first periodical, edited and published by Mrs. Eddy. Mrs. Eddy commented about the *Journal* as follows (*Miscellaneous Writings,* p. 4): "At this date, 1883, a newspaper edited and published by the Christian Scientists has become a necessity. . . . Further enlightenment is necessary for the age, and a periodical devoted to this work seems alone adequate to meet the requirement." In the same article she adds (p. 7), "Looking over the newspapers of the day, one naturally reflects that it is dangerous to live, so loaded with disease seems the very air. . . . A periodical of our own will counteract to some extent this public nuisance; for through our paper, at the price at which we shall issue it, we shall be able to reach many homes with healing, purifying thought." Thus in April 1883, she started the *Journal*. The first volume consisted of six numbers; the second volume of ten. The third volume was the first which corresponded in size to its present form. Thus from small beginnings sprang the *Journal* which now goes to all parts of the world.

Like the *Journal*, the *Christian Science Sentinel* began in Mrs. Eddy's thought as a newspaper. In a letter to Mr. William P. McKenzie, Trustee, dated August 20, 1898, she wrote, "The dignity of our cause and the good of the students demand of us to publish a weekly newspaper" (*Historical Sketches,* p. 127). It was first published as *The Christian Science Weekly,* September 1, 1898. Christian Scientists were very grateful for this little paper coming every week.

In a letter to Judge Hanna, she wrote, "Sentinel is the proper title for our Weekly. . . . Also let me prophesy 'Sentinel' and the motto with it describes the future of this newspaper. It will take that place and must *fill it* when numerous periodicals of our denomination are extant" (*Historical Sketches,* p. 127).

The first issue of the *Sentinel* under its new name appeared January 26, 1899, with its new motto, "What I say unto you I say unto all, WATCH." So we see that the words "Sentinel" and "watch" indicate the permanent position of this periodical.

Several months later Mrs. Eddy made a By-Law in regard to our periodicals which reads: "It shall be the privilege and duty of every member, who can afford it, to subscribe for the periodicals which are the organs of this Church; and it shall be the duty of the Directors to see that these periodicals are ably edited and kept abreast of the times" (*Church Manual,* p. 44).

Mrs. Eddy depended radically on divine guidance. When she felt sure that the divine Mind had spoken to her, she did not hesitate to act. Her attitude was that she had to obey God. This she did, sometimes even before she knew the reason for doing so. One instance of this occurred during the trial already referred to. As we are told in the book, *Historical Sketches,* by Judge Clifford P. Smith (p. 130), Mrs. Eddy "called a consultation of her lawyers, and found that they agreed to take a certain position which she regarded as unwise. A full discussion made no change. After they left her, she sent for Mr. Elder, told him that they were wrong, and obtained his promise that he would ask the other lawyers to reconsider the question." They did so, as Mr. Elder's daughter later recalled, with the result "that they reversed their decision, followed the lines insisted upon by Mrs. Eddy, and during the trial it became indubitably clear that she had been right."*

During my stay at Pleasant View, Mrs. Eddy often called her lawyers for interviews. Many reporters sought interviews; some were granted.

Mr. William E. Curtis of the *Chicago Record-Herald,* after an interview, made this remark, "I have never seen a woman eighty-

---

*From *The Life of Samuel J. Elder,* by Margaret M. Elder, p. 202.

six years of age with greater physical or mental vigor" (*Historical Sketches,* p. 131).

Mr. Arthur Brisbane of the *New York Evening Journal* and the *Cosmopolitan Magazine* said, "It is quite certain that nobody could see this beautiful and venerable woman and ever again speak of her except in terms of affectionate reverence and sympathy." I had the privilege of meeting these eminent editors and writers at Pleasant View.

During this trial, it seemed that every phase of evil presented itself to be met and destroyed. One day Mrs. Eddy called her students into her study and pointed to a very black cloud, shaped like a cornucopia, coming toward the house in direct line with her front study window. She asked each one to go to a window and face it, and to realize that there were no destructive elements in God's creation. Although appearing to whirl straight toward Pleasant View, a mile or so away the cyclone changed its course and went around Concord into the mountains, doing very little damage.

Mrs. Eddy had a keen, delightful sense of humor. One day while I was busy in her room, she was reading a letter; looking up, she called me and said in substance, "How do they demonstrate money and furniture?" I replied, "I do not know, I was not taught that." Then, as I recall, she said, "Thank God you were not. We demonstrate Life, Truth, and Love, and *they* give us our supplies; we do not *demonstrate* material things."

Mrs. Eddy was very fond of little children. One day she told me of a little boy and a little girl who came each May Day to hang a basket of arbutus on her door. She asked me to watch for them and bring them in to see her. I did so, and much to their embarrassment I took them up to her room. She talked lovingly to them about their school and Sunday School, and thanked them for the flowers and the love that prompted their gift. After they were gone, she asked Mr. Frye to get them each a little gold ring next time he went to Concord.

There is a sweet picture of Mrs. Eddy as the Founder, Discoverer, and Leader of Christian Science which I have retained in memory.

I see her in the early morning, dressed, ready for the day, seated in her study beside her writing desk, in the bay window, with her Bible and the textbook in her lap. Calm, serene, silently communing with divine Love, as evidenced by the faraway look in her eyes, she seemed to be looking into reality. There she was, waiting for the workers whom she had just called in for the morning talk. When all were gathered before her, she would open her Bible at random and read the first thing her eyes fell upon. Then she would give the spiritual interpretation of it, which flowed from her lips as freely as if she had written it out.

This was her bread from heaven, her inspiration and revelation, the manna for the day, which she shared with the members of her household. It was clear that because of her spirituality she was the revelator of Christian Science, its Discoverer, Founder, and Leader.

The religion which Mrs. Eddy founded is her great legacy to humanity by which mankind may choose the good and reject the evil. To reject the evil and *accept* the good is the operation or working order of Christian Science itself. Mrs. Eddy's gift to us is the revelation of the truth of being. The organization which she founded makes available to all mankind the life-giving waters of Truth. In Revelation we read, "And the Spirit and the bride say, Come. . . . And let him that is athirst come. And whosoever will, let him take the water of life freely."

The Mother Church, The First Church of Christ, Scientist, in Boston, Massachusetts, together with The Christian Science Publishing Society, and the periodicals it publishes, were founded and established by our Leader. They are safeguarded by the *Manual of The Mother Church* which, through the inspired provisions of its By-Laws, protects and preserves the Christian Science movement.

The law of true Christianity is manifest in the activities of The Mother Church. Moses gave us the moral law. Elias exemplified prophecy. Christ Jesus demonstrated the divine law in the destruction of sin, disease, and death. Mrs. Eddy gave us the Science of Christianity which forever reveals to all mankind the practical application of the divine law in everyday experience. The Mother Church, the government and laws of which are God-derived, enables each member who faithfully adheres to its teachings to be properly self-governed, for he demonstrates that God alone governs him.

Of the ideal woman it is said in Proverbs 31:26: "She openeth her mouth with wisdom; and in her tongue is the law of kindness." This certainly is descriptive of our beloved Leader and friend, Mary Baker Eddy. In her *Message to The Mother Church for 1902* she said (p. 4), "Competition in commerce, deceit in councils, dishonor in nations, dishonesty in trusts, begin with 'Who shall be greatest?' I again repeat, Follow your Leader, only so far as she follows Christ."

We know she was a faithful follower of the Christ. May her wonderful example continue to guide and illuminate our lives!

A Worker in Mrs. Eddy's Chestnut Hill Home

MARTHA W. WILCOX

The characteristic that endeared Mrs. Eddy to every member of her household was her motherliness. We never felt awed in her presence, but never for one minute were we allowed to let our thought rest upon her personality. We understood that that would be a hindrance to her. It was her instructions to us that were paramount—so much so that we could be in the house for weeks and not think of her personality. We attended to her wants and necessities, but always in our mind was what she had given us to be demonstrated. From morning till night we were busy applying the instructions she gave us to the work at hand and trying to demonstrate the truth of Christian Science.

The members of her household were not supposed to talk or discuss Christian Science at the table or among themselves. We were to live Christian Science, to be it, and not just talk the letter. This was one place in the world where the chatter about Christian Science was not heard.

Mrs. Eddy came to Chestnut Hill January 26, 1908, and I became a member of her household Monday morning, February 10, 1908—just two weeks later.

I was a very young student in Christian Science—just beginning my sixth year. And, although the Principle of Christian Science to be demonstrated was the same for all members of her household, the instructions that Mrs. Eddy gave me, and her requirements of me, were different in their degree from those who were more experienced in Christian Science practice. And it is only fair to Mrs. Eddy and to others that this be taken into consideration.

After removing my wraps, Mrs. Sargent took me into Mrs. Eddy's study and introduced me as Mrs. Wilcox from Kansas City. Mrs. Eddy said to me, "Good morning, Mrs. Wilcox, I felt your sweet presence in the house." Then she had me seated directly in front of her and asked, "What can you do?" I replied that I could do almost anything that one would do who has kept house and had a family to care for. Then she asked me, "What are you willing to do?" I replied that I was willing to do anything that she wanted me to do. Then she said, "My housekeeper has had to go home because of the illness of her father and I should like to have you take her place for the time being."

Then she began to talk to me on mental malpractice. In effect this is what she said: Sometimes a sense of a personality arises before your thought and leads you to believe that a personality is something outside and separate from your thought, that can harm you. She showed me that the real danger was never this threatened attack from outside my thought where the personality seemed to be, but that the real danger was always within my thought. She made it clear that my sense of personality was mental—a mental image formed in my so-called mortal mind and was never external or separate from my mind. This supposititious mortal mind outlined itself as a belief of a material personality with form and conditions and laws and circumstances—in fact with all the phenomena that are embraced in what is called material life or personality. And then she showed me that not one solitary fact in this whole fabric of supposititious evil was true.

She showed me that I must detect that all this mental phenomena was only aggressive mental suggestion coming to me, for me to adopt it, as my own thought.

She showed me that because mental malpractice is mental, the only place that I could meet it was within what seemed to be my own mentality and the only way that I could meet it was

Mrs. Eddy's home in Chestnut Hill

Martha W. Wilcox

to give up the belief in a power and presence other than God or Truth.

She showed me that this seeming-within enemy could never harm me if I were awake to the truth and active in the truth. This lesson on mental malpractice was quite apropos for one entering a household comprised of never less than 17 up to 25 so-called personalities.

After this talk on mental malpractice, Mrs. Eddy opened her Bible and read to me from Luke: "He that is faithful in that which is least is faithful also in much: and he that is unjust in the least is unjust also in much. If therefore ye have not been faithful in the unrighteous mammon, who will commit to your trust the true riches? And if ye have not been faithful in that which is another man's, who shall give you that which is your own?" (Luke 16:10–12.)

Mrs. Eddy, no doubt, realized that at my stage of growth, I thought of creation—that is all things—as separated into two groups, one group spiritual and the other group material, and that somehow I must get rid of the group I called material.

But during this lesson, I caught my first glimpse of the fact that all right, useful things—which I had been calling "the unrighteous mammon"—were mental and represented spiritual ideas. She showed me that unless I were faithful and orderly with the objects of sense that made up my present mode of consciousness, there could never be revealed to me the truer riches or the progressive higher revealments of substance and things.

The two lessons that I received that first morning were fundamentally great lessons.

FIRST: I was to handle mental malpractice within my own mentality.
SECOND: There are not two groups of creation—but just one.

When she had finished she said, "Now, take your young child

200

down into Egypt and let it grow up until it is strong enough to stand alone." By this I understood I was not to talk to anyone about what was given me until I had made it substance in my own thought.

You have all heard many things about Mrs. Eddy's exactness and orderliness of thought and action. She showed forth to an unusual degree the exactness and divine order of God—her Mind, and she required perfection of thought and action from those of her household.

Even the different lengths of pins had their respective corners in her pincushion and she took out the pin she needed, without taking out and putting back the different lengths. No one would have thought of changing a pin in her pincushion. Mrs. Eddy believed that if one's thought was not orderly and exact in the things that make up present consciousness, that same thought would not be exact enough to give a treatment or use an exact science.

These qualities in Mrs. Eddy's mind were very pronounced—far beyond what my so-called human mind could comprehend or sense. She taught me that the Mind I then had was God, and that I was to show forth God—my own Mind—in order and exactness and perfection.

I had not been there long until she asked me to make her bed every morning for a month and turn down the upper sheet exactly two and one half inches. She required that we place the furniture just so, and we were to express dominion in all things, and whether the potatoes to be baked were large or small, they were to be neither overdone or underdone at the proper time— and mealtime never varied a minute in her house. The meals were exactly on time.

Mrs. Eddy loved a new dress as well as any other woman. And the little lady who made her dresses, while she used a dress form, was expected to have the dresses perfect, without fittings. Mrs. Eddy knew that Mind's work and Mind always fit—they are one and the same. And the sense of anything being too large or too small was not found in Mind. Therefore, excuses or alibis were of no avail with Mrs. Eddy.

Perhaps someone is wondering what happened if an individual did not bring out perfection and exactness concretely. Mrs. Eddy clearly discerned if one were striving to show forth God—his own right Mind—in everything. But if an individual were not spiritually-minded enough to discern Mrs. Eddy's real purpose in these requirements, or thought them unnecessary, or thought Mrs. Eddy was just exacting and concerned only about the so-called material things, or did not see the necessity of being obedient—such a one did not remain long in the home.

At one time she called me to be her personal maid, and as I knew nothing about the requirements of such a position, she gave me seven pages stating the things that were to be done. These necessitated continuity of action without false moves or forgetting.

When night came and I had tucked her in bed, I said— "Mother, I did not forget once nor make a mistake, did I?" She smiled up at me from her pillow and replied, "No, you didn't." That night, about midnight, she rang my bell. I went to her and asked what she wanted. She said, "Martha, do you ever forget?" I replied, "Mother, Mind never forgets." Then she said, "Go back to bed." Mrs. Eddy always required us, whenever possible, to answer her questions with the absolute statement of Science.

The next morning after she was seated in her study, she said, "Martha, if you had admitted last night that anyone can forget, you would have made yourself liable to forgetting. Whatever error you admit in yourself as real or in another, you make yourself liable to that error. Admitting error real produces error and is all there is to it."

There was another incident that occurred while I acted in the capacity of maid to Mrs. Eddy that was a great lesson to me. It was when Mrs. Eddy wrote and added to *Science and Health* the two lines at the bottom of page 442: "Christian Scientists, be a law to yourselves that mental malpractice cannot harm you either when asleep or when awake."

She wrote almost constantly for three days. She consulted the dictionary, the grammar, studied synonyms and antonyms, and when she had finished, she had these two lines to add to *Science and Health*. I marveled at her perseverance and the time she consumed in writing two lines. But she had worked out a scientific statement for Christian Science students that would stand through the ages. After writing for three days, she gave us two lines, but who of us can estimate the value of these two lines?

Those closely associated with Mrs. Eddy knew when she was giving birth, in thought, to some important decision—such as a change in the Church, or the making of a new By-Law, or something in connection with her writings. Many times there seemed to be great travail when these things were being born of the Spirit. I remember such a time when she abolished the Communion season of The Mother Church, and again when certain new By-Laws were brought out.

In *The First Church of Christ, Scientist, and Miscellany* Mrs. Eddy has given us an instruction for Christian Science practice. The following was written in 1910—just a short time before she left us and illustrates the quality and vitality of her thought in her 90th year: "You can never demonstrate spirituality until you declare yourself to be immortal and understand that you are so. Christian Science is absolute; it is neither behind the point of perfection nor advancing towards it; it is at this point and must be practised therefrom" (p. 242). Frequently, Mrs. Eddy would say to some member of her household, "Now remember what you are."

Mrs. Eddy expected me to know where everything was in the house, even though she had not seen it, herself, for years. And, why not, when consciousness includes all. She taught me that there was only one consciousness, and that this consciousness was my consciousness and included all ideas as present and at hand and she expected me to demonstrate it.

In her personal instruction she gave nothing to me but what she has given in her writings to all students of Christian Science. But what so impressed her instructions upon my mind was that she required of me immediate application and demonstration of what she taught. Without this required application and demonstration, Mrs. Eddy knew that the instructions she gave would be of little value to me.

At one time, I was a mental worker for seven weeks. One evening she gave me a problem to work, and of course I had a great desire to prove the reality at hand, so I worked the greater part of the night.

In the morning she called me to her and said, "Martha, why did you not do your work?" I replied, "Mother, I did." She said, "No, you didn't, you had a good talk with the devil. Why did you not know God's allness?"

I said, "Mother, I tried." And her reply was, "Well, if Jesus had just tried and failed, we would have no Science today." Then she had a card hung on the inside of the door to my room on which was printed in large letters, "Faith without works is dead." I looked at that for two weeks.

When those of her household failed to make a demonstration, there was no spirit of self-justification. We felt very much as I believe the disciples felt when being taught by the Master. There were many demonstrations that we made, and many that we did not make.

During the time that I was under Mrs. Eddy's personal instruction and a mental worker, she gave us two lessons from the Scriptures that impressed me very, very much.

One was on "Animal Magnetism"—based on the narrative of the man who was born blind. She showed us very clearly that "neither hath this man sinned, nor his parents" for they were both the divine man. For a long time I clearly saw that there was no such thing as a sinning mortal man, but only the perfect man, needing no healing. I saw that my so-called matter man was the divine man—seen in reversion or seen "through a glass, darkly" as St. Paul says.

The other lesson was on "Answer to Prayer" taken from the first chapter of James, the first to eighth verses. When she read, "But let him ask in faith, nothing wavering," I clearly saw that a double-minded man could not expect to receive anything of the Lord.

Mrs. Eddy's Bible Lessons were wonderful. She usually began each morning's instruction with a lesson from the Bible. Holding her Bible between her hands, she let it open where it would and began with what her eyes first fell upon.

When Mrs. Eddy gave personal instruction, it was not given to students as in a class, nor was it continuous for a definite period of time. When Mrs. Eddy so desired, she called a student to her, or she called her group of mental workers to her, sometimes several times a day. And the individual student or the group of mental workers always stood while she instructed them.

Mrs. Eddy sometimes had guests to dinner—12 o'clock dinner. She liked to have to dinner such persons as Bliss Knapp, of whom she was very fond, Mrs. Knott, Mr. Dixon, and others with whom she had interviews.

Mr. Young was out to dinner and had an interview with Mrs. Eddy a short time before he taught the Normal class in 1910. And when he told Mrs. Eddy that "that was the best dinner that I ever ate," she expressed just as much satisfaction as any other woman would have done.

Mrs. Eddy sometimes read the advertised bargains in the Boston daily newspaper. She was always interested in the affairs of the day and especially was she interested in all inventions. At one time there was an exhibition in flying near Boston. Usually, Mrs. Eddy did not want the members of her household to be away, but on this occasion she insisted that several of us go to see these flights. Comparatively speaking, it was not much of an exhibition, but it was wonderful in that day. And to Mrs. Eddy it was the appearance of an advancing thought and she was interested in every detail of the exhibition.

The members of Mrs. Eddy's household were nearly all experienced practitioners and teachers. There was a group who did mental work, some of whom cared for the secretarial work, and saw to all correspondence.

Then there was a group of women, usually five in number, practically all of whom had left their own homes—some of whom were practitioners, and each one a good working student in Christian Science—who took care of Mrs. Eddy's entire home. We washed all the windows on the inside of the house, washed and stretched all lace curtains, and washed and ironed Mrs. Eddy's personal things. Every room in the house was carpeted and many of them with velvet carpets. These were kept in perfect condition with brooms. There were no vacuum cleaners until after I had been there several months. I think we had almost the first one that came out.

Then there was all the cooking and the planning of the meals for a family of 17 regularly, up to 25 at times. I usually went to Faneuil Hall Market twice each week to buy the meats and fish. Most of the groceries were bought at Brookline and during the summer months a Greek boy came to the house with fruits and berries and vegetables each day.

I have tried to show you something of what we did while in the house and we were busy from early morning until late at night. Mrs. Eddy's home was a very practical home. There was nothing mysterious going on, but it was necessary to have around her those who could in a small way understand her mission to the world.

About two weeks before she left us, she called me into her study about five o'clock in the evening. She was resting on her couch as she usually did before her evening meal. I wish you might have heard her expressions of gratitude for her home and her gratitude to those who were caring for her home. She commented on how clean and beautiful we were keeping it and what it meant to her to have such a place in which to do her work and carry on the movement of Christian Science.

She said, "You girls are so good to do this for me." Then she said, "Martha, is there any reason why you should not stay with me forever?" I replied, "Mother, I will stay with you as long as you need me or want me to stay."

I learned later from Mr. Frye just why Mrs. Eddy wanted my assurance that I would stay with her. Mrs. Eddy had decided that I was to go through the Normal class within a very short time and she thought that I might desire to go home and teach.

Perhaps Mrs. Eddy has best expressed her feelings about her home and the members of her household in her "Pæan of Praise," in *The First Church of Christ, Scientist, and Miscellany,* where she writes (pp. 355–356):

> "The Christian Scientists at Mrs. Eddy's home are the happiest group on earth. Their faces shine with the reflection of light and love; their footsteps are not weary; their thoughts are upward; their way is onward, and their light shines. The world is better for this happy group of Christian Scientists; Mrs. Eddy is happier because of them; God is glorified in His reflection of peace, love, joy.
>
> "When will mankind awake to know their present ownership of all good, and praise and love the spot where God dwells most conspicuously in His reflection of love and leadership?"

Biographical Notes

Parker, Mary Godfrey

Little is known about Mrs. Parker's life beyond what she tells in her reminiscence of Mrs. Eddy. In that respect her life is typical of many others that would be wholly unknown today were it not for the light that they throw on aspects of Mrs. Eddy's character and experience.

Bartlett, Julia S.

Born in East Windsor, Connecticut, in 1842, Miss Bartlett studied with Mrs. Eddy in 1880 and thereafter devoted forty-four unusually active years to the Cause of Christian Science. During the 1880's she served at various times as president of the Church of Christ, Scientist, its treasurer, member of its board of directors, and in other official capacities, while at the same time carrying on a busy career as practitioner and teacher of Christian Science. She was chosen by Mrs. Eddy as one of the original twelve First Members of The Mother Church when it was formed in 1892, and continued as a First or Executive Member until the office was abolished in 1908. For a fuller account, see Clifford P. Smith, *Historical Sketches* (The Christian Science Publishing Society, 1941), pages 221–229.

Blackman, C. Lulu

Following her study with Mrs. Eddy in 1885, Miss Blackman became a Christian Science practitioner and continued in that work over many decades. Her reminiscence was written in 1929 and was first published in 1950.

Thompson, Abigail Dyer

Miss Thompson had a long career as a practitioner and teacher of Christian Science in Minneapolis, Minnesota. Her mother, Emma A. Thompson, who had first met Mrs. Eddy in Portland, Maine, in the early 1860's when both were patients of Phineas P. Quimby, studied with the Leader of Christian Science in 1886 and subsequently carried on a highly successful career as a Christian Science practitioner and teacher in Minneapolis. As a young woman, Abigail Thompson was one of the sixty-five students chosen by Mrs. Eddy for her last class, held in Concord, New Hampshire in 1898. She continued in her work for the next half century.

Knott, Annie M.

Born in Scotland in 1850, young Annie Macmillan moved with her family to Canada in the 1860's, returned to England after her marriage, and finally settled in Chicago in 1882. Becoming interested in Christian Science soon after that, she took two courses at the Massachusetts Metaphysical College with Mrs. Eddy, launched public Christian Science services in Detroit, joined The Mother Church when it was formed, and for almost fifty years thereafter continued in the practice and teaching of Christian Science. In 1898 she became a member of The Christian Science Board of Lectureship, from 1903 to 1919 was Assistant or Associate Editor of the movement's religious periodicals, and from 1919 to 1934 served as the first woman member of The Christian Science Board of Directors since the forming of The Mother Church in 1892.

Gale, Frank Walter

After helping to introduce Christian Science in San Diego, California, in 1887 and studying with Mrs. Eddy in 1888, Frank Gale moved back to his home city of San Francisco, where he became a charter member of First Church of Christ, Scientist, in 1895. For the next fifty years he remained in that city, teaching and practicing Christian Science. In 1922 he was chosen to teach the Normal class in the Board of Education in Boston.

Newman, Emma Easton

When only seventeen years old, Emma Easton went through Mrs. Eddy's March Primary class of 1889 with her parents. Two years later she was listed as a practitioner in *The Christian Science Journal*. In 1893–94 her father, the Reverend D. A. Easton, served as Pastor of The Mother Church. In 1899 Miss Easton helped to organize First Church of Christ, Scientist, Cambridge, Massachusetts, and became its first Second Reader. After her marriage, she moved to Los Angeles, California, where she remained as a busy practitioner and teacher until 1950. Her reminiscence was given as a talk at The Mother Church in 1940.

Robertson, Annie Louise

Mrs. Robertson was living in Germany when she first heard of Christian Science but returned to Boston soon afterward. In 1892 her name appeared in *The Christian Science Journal* as a practitioner, and for two years (1894–96) she lived in Mrs. Eddy's former house at 385 Commonwealth Avenue with Judge and Mrs. Septimus J. Hanna. Mrs. Robertson was a member of Mrs. Eddy's last class in 1898 and for several decades was a practitioner and teacher of Christian Science in Boston.

Adams, George Wendell

A native of Kingston, Massachusetts, and educated at Phillips Exeter Academy in New Hampshire, Mr. Adams attended Christian Science services at Chickering Hall in Boston when only fifteen years old. In 1896, while still a young man, he helped organize First Church of Christ, Scientist, in Plymouth, Massachusetts, and two years later went through Mrs. Eddy's last class in Concord, becoming a teacher afterward. In 1922 he was appointed Clerk of The Mother Church, and from 1925 to 1953 served as a member of The Christian Science Board of Directors.

Lathrop, John C.

As a boy of fourteen, John Lathrop began to study Christian Science when his mother, Laura Lathrop, was healed by it. Soon afterward Mrs. Lathrop went through the Primary and Normal classes with Mrs. Eddy and moved with her family to New York City. For several years she and her son served respectively as First and Second Reader of Second Church of Christ, Scientist, in that city. Later John Lathrop was First Reader in the same church and then served The Mother Church as First Reader (1911–14) and as President (1914–15). From 1918 to 1924 he was a member of the Board of Lectureship; after this he spent a number of years practicing and teaching Christian Science in Brookline, Massachusetts.

McKenzie, Daisette D. S.

As a young woman, Daisette Stocking was a charter member of First Church of Christ, Scientist, Cleveland, Ohio. Early in the 1890's she moved to Toronto, Ontario, where she served first as pastor then as Second Reader of one of the branch churches there. Some years previous to this she had been instrumental in bringing a young Scots-Canadian Presbyterian ex-minister, William P. McKenzie, into Christian Science, and in 1901, three years after he had become a Trustee of The Christian Science Publishing Society in Boston, the two were married. Both were in Mrs. Eddy's 1898 class. In 1932 Mr. McKenzie became a Director of The Mother Church and, because of his new duties, gave up his work as a Christian Science teacher, whereupon Mrs. McKenzie held her first class and continued teaching until 1952. In 1943–44 she served as President of The Mother Church.

Mims, Sue Harper

Born in Mississippi, Sue Harper in 1866 married Major Livingston Mims of Atlanta, Georgia, who served for some years as Mayor of that city. Mrs. Mims was widely known through the South as a hostess and civic leader. Learning of Christian Science, she was taught by Julia Bartlett in 1886, later became a Christian Science practitioner and teacher, and from 1898 to 1911 addressed audiences across the country as a member of The Christian Science Board of Lectureship. A contemporary tribute in the *Atlanta Constitution* stated: "Mrs. Mims is one of the brightest minds of the entire South without regard to sex, and Christian Science won its most formidable exponent in this section when she became an advocate of its doctrines."

Shipman, Emma C.

As a young woman recently out of college, Miss Shipman joined The Mother Church in 1893 and five years later was chosen as a member of Mrs. Eddy's last class. During the sixty years that followed she was active in Boston as a practitioner and teacher and for some time was a member of the Bible Lesson Committee. In 1949–50 she was President of The Mother Church and in 1952 taught the Normal class for the Board of Education.

Stewart, Mary

Like Emma Shipman, Mrs. Stewart became interested in Christian Science shortly after finishing college, joined The Mother Church in 1893, and was chosen for Mrs. Eddy's 1898 class. Afterward she moved to Chicago and had an active career as practitioner and teacher there for the next half century.

Hill, Calvin C.

After meeting Mrs. Eddy in 1899, Mr. Hill became a First Member of The Mother Church in 1901. The following year he went through the Normal class of the Board of Education under Edward A. Kimball. He was made Sunday School superintendent of The Mother Church in that same year and held the position for fourteen years. He also served on the Finance Committee of the Church for almost the entire period from 1902 to 1943.

Knapp, Bliss

In 1903, two years after graduation from college, Mr. Knapp had Primary class instruction, and in 1907 Normal class. Meanwhile he had been placed on the Board of Lectureship in 1904 and continued as a lecturer until 1922. In 1912 and again in 1927 he served as President of The Mother Church and in 1923–26 as its First Reader. After another short stint as lecturer, he devoted himself wholly to his work in Boston as a Christian Science practitioner and teacher.

McKee, Clara Knox

Mrs. McKee joined The Mother Church in 1893 and served as Second Reader of First Church of Christ, Scientist, Scranton, Pennsylvania, a few years later. Called to Pleasant View, Concord, New Hampshire, in August 1906, to serve as Mrs. Eddy's personal maid, she remained in that capacity until July 1907.

Wilcox, Martha W.

Formerly a schoolteacher in Kansas, Mrs. Wilcox returned to Kansas City after her period of service at Mrs. Eddy's home in Chestnut Hill and her attendance at the Normal class held in Boston in December 1910. For the rest of her life she was active as a Christian Science practitioner and teacher in her home city.

Index

Adams, George Wendell,
  biographical notes, 211–212
  reminiscences, 107–110
Animal magnetism, 48, 57–58
Armstrong, Joseph, 19–21, 84

Baker, Mark, 185
Bartlett, Julia,
  biographical notes, 209
  reminiscences, 28–52
Bates, Edward P., 83
Baum, Louise M., 95
Benson, Nancy, 8–9
Bible Lessons, 103–104, 123
Bible, quoted or referred to, 40–41, 43,
    47, 50, 54–56, 58–61, 69, 72–73,
    78, 83, 90, 96, 101, 108, 110, 112,
    115–116, 120–123, 125, 127–128,
    132, 134–137, 139, 141–142, 144,
    152, 160–162, 174, 180, 182, 184,
    187, 189, 191, 194–195, 200,
    204–205
Blackman, C. Lulu,
  biographical notes, 209
  reminiscences, 53–62
Boston Globe, The, 183
Bow, New Hampshire, 81
Branch churches, 103
Brisbane, Arthur, 193
Bush, Rev. R. Perry, 18
Buswell, Ezra M., 108, 127–128

Chase, Stephen, 84
Chestnut Hill (Mrs. Eddy's home),
  household, 196–207
  move to, 116–117
  study, 177

Chicago exhibition, 122
Chicago Inter-Ocean, 152
Chicago Record-Herald, 192
Chickering Hall, Boston, 16, 63–64,
    103–104
Christ and Christmas by Mrs. Eddy, 97, 124
Christian Healing by Mrs. Eddy, 33
Christian Science Board of Lectureship,
  The, 82
Christian Science Hall, 99–100, 107–110,
    127–146
Christian Science Journal, The,
  editing of, 84–86
  established, 123–124
  quoted, 143–144, 159–160
Christian Science Monitor, The,
  established, 124
  quoted, 95–96
Christian Science periodicals,
  editing of, 84–86
Christian Science Sentinel,
  editing of, 84–86
  established, 19, 191–192
  quoted, 150–152, 171–172
Christian Science Series, 146
Christian Science Weekly, see Christian Science
    Sentinel
Christ Jesus, 29–30, 58, 61, 70–71, 73, 80,
    85, 96, 106, 108, 111, 119–120, 125,
    132, 134, 137, 141–142, 147–149,
    151–152, 161, 180, 182, 184–185,
    187, 189, 195, 204
Church Manual, see Manual of The Mother
    Church
Church of Christ, Scientist, The,
  see Mother Church, The
Church, Walter L., 170

Class instruction, see Eddy, Mary Baker,
    teacher
Clergyman, reverses his view of Christian
    Science, 121–122
"Communion address" by Mrs. Eddy, 152
Conant, Mr. and Mrs. Albert, 17
Confidentiality, 98, 107–108, 117
Congregations, Christian Science,
    103–104
Cook, Eliza, 177
Corser, Bartlett, 97–98
Corser, Rev. Enoch, 97–98
Cosmopolitan Magazine, 193
C. S. B. and C. S. D. certificates, 144
Curtis, William, 192

Dixon, Frederick, 205
Dunmore, Lady, 83

Eddy, Asa Gilbert, 1–4, 7–8, 30–31,
    34–35, 37–39
Eddy, Mary Baker,
    Bible, use of, 43, 83–84, 101, 112,
        115, 135–136, 144, 182, 194
    characteristics of, 89, 93–94, 96, 98,
        104, 106, 108, 111–115, 129–132,
        136–138, 140–141, 154, 176, 193,
        196, 201
    character, need to understand her,
        103, 136–137
    Chestnut Hill, move to, 116–117
    children, love for, 99, 193
    comments on:
        animal magnetism, 94, 204–205
        error, 42, 80, 95, 113, 142, 202
        evil, 58, 76–77, 80, 117, 134, 143,
            148
        gifts, 138
        heal, how to, 68, 89–90, 110, 118,
            134, 143, 147–148
        healing works, demands, 57, 132
        healings, keeping record of, 65
        home, 142
        human philosophy, 109–110
        humor, value of, 109–110, 142
        love, importance of, 89, 101, 143
        mental malpractice, 73, 197–200
        mount of transfiguration, 141–142
        note-taking, 56, 94
        relationship between God and
            man, 108–109, 137–138
        salvation, 60
        speaking distinctly, 109, 137, 140
        spiritualism, comments on, 72–73
        students, choosing, 144
        supply, 134, 137–138, 193
        teaching, method of, 89–91, 94,
            109–110, 131, 142
        trinity, definition of, 142
        truth, revelation of, 132
    Concord, N.H., move to, 48
    confidentiality, insistence on, 47–48,
        98, 107–108, 117, 127
    current affairs, interest in, 205
    daily metaphysical work, 173
    description of, 13, 24, 41–42, 55,
        59–60, 63–65, 71, 93, 108, 114, 130,
        146, 152–154, 182, 194
    drives, daily, 61, 99, 115–116, 148
    fan, lesson on, 186–187
    gifts:
        from followers, 94, 154, 175–176,
            178–179
        to followers, 154, 180
    healer, 5–6, 9–10, 42–43, 45–46, 67–68,
        106, 132–133, 147–148
    humor, sense of, 94, 98–99, 115–116,
        135, 142, 176, 178, 182, 193
    hymn, strengthened by, 186
    judging people, 86
    letters:
        from, 54, 75, 82, 90–91, 96–98, 119,
            126, 139–140, 147, 162,
            164–165, 173–182, 188–189,
            191–192
        to, 54, 159–160, 178, 180
    marries Asa Eddy, 82
    metaphysics, verify in *Science and
        Health,* 66, 160–161
    "Mother" to early followers, 96, 106, 160
    Nashes, association with, 4–12
    ordained as pastor of the Church of
        Christ, Scientist, 35–36
    orderliness, insistence on, 113,
        129–130, 179, 201

Eddy, Mary Baker (*continued*)
    Pastor, appoints impersonal, 103–104,
        123
    portraits of, 64, 114
    preaching:
        "Communion address," 152
        in original Mother Church, 48–50,
            104–105
        on Psalm 91, 60
    reading in churches, views on,
        113–114
    rubber band in shape of heart, story of,
        157–160
    scholastic theology, dissatisfaction
        with, 101
    teacher, class instruction:
        class of 1880, 31–32
        class of 1885, 54–62
        class of 1887 (Normal), 46, 70–74
        class of 1888, 87–90
        class of 1889, 93–95
        class of 1898 (last class), 99–101,
            108–111, 128–145, 148–149
    writer:
        appraisals of, 95–96, 122
        Science and Health, 120–121,
            202–203
*Editorial Comments on the Life and Work
    of Mary Baker Eddy,* 122
Elder, Samuel J., 192
Elias, 195

Farlow, Alfred, 25
Fincastle, Lord, 83
*First Church of Christ, Scientist, and
    Miscellany, The,* by Mrs. Eddy,
    quoted, 87, 102, 120–121, 139–140,
        162, 171–172, 183, 185, 190, 203,
        207
First Church of Christ, Scientist, The,
    Boston, Massachusetts, see
    Mother Church, The
Foster, Dr. Ebenezer J., 15
Frye, Calvin, 40–41, 47–48, 67, 73, 89,
    108, 154–155, 162, 164, 186–187,
    207

Fuller, Chief Justice Melville Weston, 26

Gale, Frank Walter,
    biographical notes, 210–211
    reminiscences, 87–92
Glover, George, Jr., 14–15
Glover, Mary Baker, see Eddy, Mary
    Baker
Godfrey, Christiana, 1–27
Godfrey, George Llewellyn, 1–27
Golden Rule, 180, 183

Hanna, Judge Septimus J., 116, 128, 133,
    136, 143, 167, 191
Hanna, Mrs. Septimus J., 116, 128
Hawthorne Hall, 40
Healings, 5–6, 9–10, 29–32, 42–43,
    45–46, 53, 57–58, 66–68, 70–71,
    74–75, 87, 105–106, 147, 150–152,
    167–171
Hill, Calvin,
    biographical notes, 213–214
    reminiscences, 150–183
Historical Sketches, 191–193
Human Life magazine, 26

Jesus, see Christ Jesus
Johnson, William B., 18, 84
John the Baptist, 184
"Joy cometh in the morning," 186

"Key Flower" by Bayard Taylor, lesson
    from, 187–189
Kimball, Edward, 139, 214
Kimball, Mr. and Mrs. Edward, 128
Kimball, W. B. C. (photographer), 114
Knapp, Bliss,
    as guest, 205
    biographical notes, 214
    reminiscences, 184–189
Knott, Annie,
    as guest, 205
    biographical notes, 210
    reminiscences, 70–86

Lathrop, John C.,
  biographical notes, 212
  reminiscences, 111–118
Lea, Charles Herman, 122
Life of Mary Baker Eddy, The,
  by Sibyl Wilbur, 93, 97
Lincoln, Elsie, 50–51
Lord's Prayer, 55
Lynn, Number 8 Broad Street, 3

Mann, John F., 169
Mann, Joseph, 165–166
  first healing in Christian Science,
    167–171
Mann, Pauline, 165–166, 170
Manual of The Mother Church, By-Laws,
  117–118, 123, 182, 192, 194
Massachusetts Metaphysical College,
  37–51
Maynell, Lewis, 26–27
McKee, Clara Knox,
  biographical notes, 212
  reminiscences, 190–195
McKenzie, Daisette D. S.,
  biographical notes, 212
  reminiscences, 119–126
McKenzie, William P., 191
McLellan, Archibald, 84
Message to The Mother Church for 1902
  by Mrs. Eddy, quoted, 195
Mims, Sue Harper,
  biographical notes, 213
  reminiscences, 127–138
Miscellaneous Writings by Mrs. Eddy,
  quoted, 59, 61, 63, 91–92, 94–95,
  97, 123–124, 132, 143, 148,
  161–162, 183, 190–191
Monkeys, the three brass, 117
Mother Church, The:
  construction of Extension, 103
  construction of Original Edifice, 103
  first members, 104
  Mrs. Eddy preaches in, 48–50,
    104–105, 152
Mother's Room, 12–13, 20, 48, 105

Nash, Mr. and Mrs. William, 4–6, 9, 21
National Christian Scientist Association,
  75, 77–78
Neal, James, 153
New Hampshire State Fair, 22, 115–116
Newman, Emma Easton,
  biographical notes, 211
  reminiscences, 93–101
New York Evening Journal, 193
"Next Friends" suit, 124, 180–182, 190,
  192–193
Nunn, Henry D., 23

O'Brien, Sibyl Wilbur, 25–26, 93, 97
"Old Arm-Chair, The" (poem), 177

Parker, Danforth P. W., 16–24
Parker, Mary Godfrey,
  biographical notes, 209
  reminiscences, 1–27
Pastor, Bible and *Science and Health*
  ordained as, 103–104, 123
Patterson, Mary M., see Eddy, Mary Baker
Plea for Christian Science, A, by C. H. Lea,
  122
Pleasant View (Mrs. Eddy's home), 111
  balcony address by Mrs. Eddy, 23, 83, 91,
    114–115
  household, 111–118, 171–173
  move from, 116–117
Poems by Mrs. Eddy, quoted, 110
Practice, Christian Science, entering,
  32–34, 40–41
Pulpit and Press by Mrs. Eddy, quoted, 149

Reading in churches, 113–114
Reading Rooms, Christian Science,
  124–125
Retrospection and Introspection by
  Mrs. Eddy, quoted, 101
Robertson, Annie Louise,
  biographical notes, 211
  reminiscences, 102–106
Roosevelt, President Theodore, 26

Sargent, Laura, 80, 153, 155, 197

Science and Health with Key to the Scriptures by Mrs. Eddy,
quoted, 57–59, 60–61, 68, 80, 102, 108–110, 111, 113, 124, 131, 141, 144, 157, 161, 164, 183, 185, 187, 202–203
revision of, 121
study of, 91
writing of, 120–121, 202–203

Sermon on the Mount, 110, 144, 152

Shipman, Emma C.,
biographical notes, 213
reminiscences, 139–145

"Signs of the Heart" (poem), 158

Smith, Hanover P., 37

Smith, Judge Clifford P., 192

Steinert Hall, Boston, 79

Stewart, Isabella M., 79

Stewart, Mary,
biographical notes, 213
reminiscences, 146–149

Streeter, Gen. Frank, 181

Swinton's Fourth Reader, 187

Taylor, Bayard, 187

Ten Commandments, 110, 142, 144

Thompson, Abigail Dyer,
biographical notes, 210
reminiscences, 63–69

Tremont Temple, 21, 76, 83, 105

Trinity, letter from Mary Baker Eddy on, 142

Unity of Good by Mrs. Eddy, quoted, 58, 94, 148

Whiting, Abbie K., 32–33, 36–37, 39

Whiting, Lilian, 152

Wilbur, Sibyl, 25–26, 93, 97

Wilcox, Martha W.,
biographical notes, 214
reminiscences, 196–207

Willis, John B., 84

World's Parliament of Religions, Chicago, 122

Wright, Maude, 21